Becoming the
Vendor
of Choice

The Secrets to
Powerful Retail Relationships

Rick Segel

Specific
House
PUBLISHING

Published by:
Specific House Publishing
543 Davinci Pass
Kissimmee, FL 34759

Requests for permission should be sent to:
Specific House Publishing
543 Davinci Pass
Kissimmee, FL 34759
781-272-9995
800-814-7998
800-847-9411 (fax)
Email: Rick@RickSegel.com
Web: www.RickSegel.com

Printed in the United States of America

ISBN: 9781934683019

Library of Congress Control Number: 2008910197

Dedication

I would like to dedicate this book to all those vendors and manufacturers who work hard every day to improve the lives of retailers. You are the resources who understand that supplying goods or services to a retailer is a partnership. You know that being a good partner means working at the relationship, always looking for new ideas and finding the courage to keep trying them.

To my family — Lori, Keith, Shawn, Jason, Thomas, Lisa F., Mike, Alexis, TJ, Andy, Lisa S., and Jillian — I dedicate this book so they will some day know that their grandparents tried to make a difference in the world and make it just a little better place for us all to live in. That commitment is part of who my grandchildren are and what they will become.

To my wife, partner, soul mate, lover, and best friend, Margie — who shares in all of the work but rarely gets the credit — I dedicate this book and every book I will ever write. Margie is the person behind the scenes, the director, producer, critic, and encourager. She is the one who makes it all possible, without pomp or flair but with a quiet (sometimes not so quiet) "let's make it work" approach that helps me turn ideas into dreams and dreams into reality.

Preface

Rick Segel thinks like a retailer, acts like a retailer, and understands the highs and lows a retailer feels. This is because he has been on the front line of the retail experience. Rick is from Boston and has 25 years of experience in specialty retailing as owner of one of New England's most successful independent women's specialty stores. During his retailing career, Rick was invited to write articles for a number of trade publications — invitations that eventually gave birth to an independent writing, speaking, and consulting career.

Rick has spoken to retail and vendor groups over 1,900 times in 49 states and in eight countries. The reason Rick wrote this book is because of a series of questions he was constantly receiving. The question always began in a similar fashion with a rhetorical "You were a retailer" or "You talk to retailers all the time." Then came the real question: *How can I do more business with them?*

Each time, the questioner quickly added the qualifier: That's without giving it away. Translation: *How can I increase my business with retailers without reducing my prices?*

As Rick shared solutions in responding to the sales reps and manufacturers, he came to realize that even the most basic suggestion offered was received with amazement.

Typical response: "I never thought of that!"

This nearly universal thirst for common solutions gave rise to his first book on the relationship between vendors and retailers called *How to Become the Preferred Vendor*. The book was a collection of those solutions — each one is a tested idea that really works. *Becoming the Vendor of Choice* was created to further explore the possibilities for both vendors and retailers in greater depth.

The purpose of this book is to be a solid source of ideas, strategies, tactics, and concepts that you can adopt and adapt to the needs of your retailers. The ultimate goal is to reposition you, the vendor, as a valued must-have resource in the eyes of your customers.

As Rick circulated drafts of *Becoming the Vendor of Choice* to sales reps for preliminary feedback, he discovered that his ideas got his readers' creative juices flowing, and they began using these ideas immediately. The strategy each vendor actually used had its roots in one of Rick's ideas, but it was his or her own creation. The expression Rick hears most often after someone reads this book is:

"We took your idea on _____ and added _____ or changed _____, and it worked perfectly for us. Thanks for the idea."

At first Rick thought this outcome was not good. But soon he realized that his main purpose was met— to stimulate thought. As one manufacturer told Rick, "Your ideas got me thinking the right way, and I had the solution I needed in no time." That is why he purposely made this book and its recommendations as user-friendly as possible, keeping each idea short, to the point, and workable.

Stimulating thought is the ultimate goal of education. An important premise behind this book is the power of education. People like to do business with those who know what they are talking about. For one thing, your ability to give retailers needed information and expertise deflects attention away from price. For another, today's need for expertise is greater than ever. There is so much to learn to keep up in the industry.

But the main reason for writing *Becoming the Vendor of Choice* is that vendors and industries that adopt a pro-education agenda toward their market are always the winners and leaders. Rick hopes you are inspired to the point of adopting several of his ideas for reaching your market more effectively, thereby enabling your retailers to reach their markets. Transform these ideas, change them, disagree with them—but at least consider them, because they have the potential to change your business forever. Rick challenges you to greatness. In return, if he inspires a great idea, please pass that along to him. Enjoy, and keep working to improve your business and the business of your retailers.

Table of Contents

CHAPTER ONE

The Complexity of Simplicity

Make your product easier to buy
than your competition,
or you will find your customers
buying from them, not you.
– Mark Cuban –

I hear a lot of questions in my role as a retail author and professional speaker. As I travel around the world, I talk to business owners large and small, vendors of every persuasion, and more sales reps than you can shake a stick at. One question is constant. No matter where I go or who I'm talking to, somebody's sure to ask the following:

"How can I increase my business with retailers without reducing my prices?"

It's a great question, and one that is a little tricky to answer. You see, the answer to this question has two parts. Part one I can tell you in a single sentence, while the second part requires the rest of this book to explain.

The first part of the answer to the *how can I increase my business with retailers without reducing my prices?* question is this:

"If you want to increase your business with retailers, you need to become the vendor of choice."

How do you become the vendor of choice — the preferred vendor, the vendor that retailers turn to time and time again when they need to place an order? That's part two of the answer. Building and reinforcing a relationship with your retailers is critical. One of the strongest reasons a retailer opts for one vendor over another comes down to nothing more and nothing less than the relationship the retailer has with that vendor. The better the relationship, the more likely the retailer is to give that vendor his business! That's why it is critical to be the vendor of choice! Luckily, there are multiple routes you can take to reach this coveted position.

In these pages, I've combined what I've learned in my twenty-five years as an independent retailer with the wisdom of some of the most successful vendors that I know. These experts come from a number of industries—from fine apparel to trash removal—but their wisdom is universal.

Together, we've created a solid source of ideas, tactics, and concepts that you can adapt to the needs of your retailers, thereby repositioning you, the vendor, as a valued must-have resource in the eyes of your customers.

☞ What Makes One Vendor a Favorite?

Retailers select vendors based on a number of criteria. Quality and selection of products are important, obviously, as is price — yet neither of these factors is of paramount importance. The single most critical factor a retailer considers when selecting vendors, whether consciously or unconsciously, is his relationship with the vendor.

The easiest way to strengthen your relationship with a retailer is to be of value to him. What is of value to retailers? The answer is obvious: concrete ways to improve their business, so they can run their store easier, more efficiently, and more profitably.

There are a number of ways you can do this, and that's what this book is about. From advertising to e-commerce, there are a lot of areas where retailers need assistance. If your organization is the one that can provide that assistance, you're establishing yourself as a valuable resource for the retailer. This is the single most critical component in becoming the vendor of choice. People like to do business with those who know what they are talking about. Today's need for expertise is greater than ever. There is so much to learn to keep up in the industry.

☞ Think Like a Retailer

To become a retailer's favorite vendor, the vendor of choice, it really helps if you understand where the retailer is coming from. There's a fundamental disconnect between most manufacturers' reps and salespeople. There's little, if any, mutual understanding. The day-to-day operation of a store and the challenges retailers face on an ongoing basis seldom enter the conversation.

Changing that is the first step to improving your relationship with your retailers. After all, the better you understand your customers, the better you can help meet their needs. So let's begin this journey with a look at an average day in the life of a retailer.

☞ One Day in the Life of a Retailer

The day starts early—the only time the delivery truck bringing the special sale merchandise can make it is a few scant minutes after the sun has risen. Guess who's got to be there to receive it?

After checking in the merchandise, our retailer tosses the invoices onto his desk. He'll have to deal with them in a little bit—but for now, there are other things to do. When the crew closed up last night, they neglected to straighten the front display. It looks like a bomb hit it, and that'll never do.

That didn't take too long—and good thing! The window displays need to be changed to reflect the new sales event. Setting up the window wasn't too bad, although the mannequins are definitely putting on weight. He didn't remember them ever being that heavy before.

That's done just in time for the first member of his sales staff to arrive. Kind of strange for her to come in twenty minutes early.

Or maybe not so strange, as she was just stopping by to let him know, amid much coughing and sneezing, that she wouldn't be in at all. She was headed over to the health center instead.

Four phone calls later our retailer manages to find a staffer who wants some extra hours. She'll be in—in an hour, after she gets her kids over to daycare.

This shouldn't be a problem. Mornings are usually slow.

Except, of course, for today. Two customers come in first thing, which wouldn't have been bad, except for the fact that they were followed by an advertising salesperson from the local shopper who would just not get a clue and leave.

Another two customers arrive, and then his sales help shows up. They work flat out all morning and manage to get some of the new sale merchandise out and on the floor. The phone rings sixteen times before lunch—three of the calls are from his sick employee, but all the rest are sales solicitations and customer queries. Most of those could be handled quickly enough, except for one disgruntled customer who not only wanted a refund but apparently wanted our retailer to crawl through ground glass to remedy an incorrect special order.

This doesn't leave our retailer with much of an appetite, but he does manage to grab a few bites of a sandwich while filing the morning's invoices and looking over the previous day's sales numbers.

Then there is a small burst of business and a visit from one of our retailer's favorite reps. Nice guy, but he likes to talk. Normally our retailer does too, but with the shop so busy the meeting got cut kind of short. Our retailer knows he agreed to try out some new merchandise, but he's not exactly sure what it is or how much he should be expecting.

He scrawls a note reminding him to call the rep and confirm the order. This note gets put in his pocket and promptly forgotten as a very loyal, and very demanding, customer comes in for her weekly visit. She always insists on dealing with our retailer, rather than any of the sales staff, so there goes another half hour of the day.

There's just enough time to make a quick run to the bank, and then the evening sales staff comes in. Our retailer takes a few minutes to discuss the way the store was left the previous evening and elicits promises that things will be better tomorrow.

Then the strip mall manager knocks on the door. Apparently some kids vandalized the trash dumpsters out back, and he wants all the store owners to come out and give a statement to the police officer.

By the time that's over, our retailer is more than ready to call it a day. He pokes his head into the office just long enough to check the store's e-mail and issue one more reminder about tidying up the store before closing time.

It's time to head for home, just in time for a very late dinner. Our retailer is exhausted. He's out cold as soon as his head hits the pillow. Tomorrow morning will be here before he knows it.

The scenario described here might be a little worse than the average retailer's day — or it might be a little better. Running a store is hard work, and it consumes a lot of time and energy. Yet when you read through this typical day, you'll see that no matter how busy our retailer is, there are some things he's not doing.

☞ What's Not in This Picture?

You might notice that the retailer hasn't gotten out of the shop. There hasn't been time to shop his competition. He doesn't know how Store X is displaying the latest shipment of widgets, nor what kind of advertising Store Y is using to draw the crowds.

We didn't hear anything about web-based sales. Paperwork and inventory control procedures seem to be rudimentary. There's a lot of room for improvement here, and you can be the one to make things better.

☞ What You Can Do for Your Retailers – and How It Helps You

Vendors enjoy a unique position. They have a perspective that many retailers don't have — although they would certainly like to. Manufacturers' reps and sales professionals aren't tied down to one store. That's one of the benefits of being on the road all the time. You have the chance to see things that the retailers don't see. You can talk to people the retailers just don't meet.

When you see five, ten, or twenty-five stores in a week, you notice things that other people don't see. You can view things with a critical eye, and can form a frame of reference based on real-life experience that your retailers just can't get. You're on the cutting edge of industry trends, often knowing what's new and exciting before almost anyone else.

Remember: Helping your retailers helps you. When the stores that sell your products prosper and thrive, your organization does better. This is one instance where, to twist the old truism a bit, it's possible to teach a man to fish — and have him feed you for a lifetime! Vendors and industries that adopt a pro-education agenda toward their market are always the winners and leaders!

☞ Be the Bottom-line Resource

"We're a bottom-line resource!" How many times have you said that line to retailers, attempting to convince them that if only they'd carry your lines or spotlight your merchandise, they'd make more money?

The truth is that if you want to position yourself as a bottom-line resource, you need to truly be a bottom-line resource. That means changing the rules of the game. Simply providing top quality merchandise at great prices isn't enough anymore. You have to do more.

It's time for retailers to look for ways to increase their sales by 20 percent and stop looking for ways to cut their costs by 20 percent. THE SAME IS TRUE FOR VENDORS. If you want to increase your sales by 20 percent, you need to adopt new selling techniques.

Becoming the true bottom-line resource — the one vendor that will help retailers sell 20 percent more, all the time — is the way for you to realize this goal!

☞ Stand out from the Crowd

Focusing on getting to know your retailers, actively adopting a pro-education agenda, and going the extra mile to help your retailers have a better, stronger business does require some effort on your part. However, it pays off — in more than one way.

Working to position yourself as the vendor of choice will differentiate your organization from the host of companies competing for the same market share. You'll stand out from the crowd as a unique company. Sure, 45 vendors might be trying to sell widgets, but you're the company that packages those widgets with an extra-value-added bonus, delivered in the form of your enhanced relationship with your retailer.

People do business based on a number of factors. One of the largest factors is the relationship they have with the vendor, both on a personal and professional level. Everything you can do to enhance this relationship will increase the likelihood that the retailer will turn to you time and time again. You are becoming the vendor of choice.

☞ Never Miss a Trick

Any time an author writes a book, there's research involved. It's part and parcel of what we do. For this book, I reached out to some of the best and brightest in the world, from companies of every size. You'll find wisdom in here that comes from reps for multi-national mega corporations — and from the rep who handles all of the T-shirt sales in a swanky resort region. It's great stuff, from great people, and I learned a lot while gathering it.

But there's one lesson I learned from a surprising source. It didn't come from any of the folks you'll read about in these pages. It came from all the people who declined interview invitations, with a polite "no, thank you" or shrugged shoulders.

Now, I'm a personable fellow. Some have even said charming. My books regularly show up on business bestseller lists, and I'm relatively confident that this will as well. I was offering vendors a chance to have their name and wisdom included in a positive setting in a high-profile book. All it would have cost them was a half-hour of their time. Yet they said no.

What does this say?

Well, it might be that I'm not as charming or personable as I might think. That's a possibility. But let's give me the benefit of the doubt — it is my book, after all! — and say that I'm at least as charming and personable as the average person.

That leaves only one answer: The vendors did not see how they would benefit from being included in the book. Seeing no immediate payoff, they declined.

That's the type of short-term, narrow thinking that plagues manufacturers' reps and sales representatives. By focusing only on the immediate benefit — today's sale, for example — other, more vital components that may take longer to develop are being ignored.

Building relationships with your customers takes time. Establishing yourself as the vendor who has not only the products, but the information, customer support, prestige, and personality that deserves preferred status takes time.

Not everything you do as a vendor will have an immediate payoff. Providing sales training to your retailers' floor staff or compiling a library of advertising images might not result in greater profitability in the next month, or the next three months, or even the next six months.

You have to ask yourself, as an organization, if you're in this for the long term, or the next six months. Not only

Do you have to make that decision as an organization, you need to make it the guiding philosophy for all of your sales team. That way, when your rep is faced with a decision, such as to participate in an interview or to follow up on tradeshow leads, she won't choose based upon what benefits her right that minute.

This may require a shift in thinking. We're trained, as a society and a culture, to focus on the here and now. If I could have everyone who's reading this book come away with only one lesson, it would be this: Abandon the idea of selling just for today. Focus on tomorrow. Put an emphasis on relationship-building and discovering what you can do to help the retailer succeed.

Opportunities to strengthen your relationship with retailers and position yourself as an attractive vendor don't come gift-wrapped and labeled. Learning to recognize and take advantage of these chances takes time, but it does get easier with practice. The world's most successful vendors don't miss a trick. When there's a chance to raise their company's visibility, display their expertise in the public sphere, and reinforce their commitment to their customers, they jump on it.

So should you.

☞ Starting the Partnership — How to Get Your Retailers to Participate

As you read through this book, you're going to find lots of suggestions for things to do with your retailers, programs to offer their employees, resources to provide for their use, and more.

All of which might make you scratch your head and say, "Yeah…great. The guys I see, day in and day out, week after week after week, are never, ever going to do that."

You're introducing a new concept to them: that as a vendor, you're a valuable partner and a provider of more than just merchandise. This will require a little selling on your part.

Educational marketing is one of the most powerful trends today. Your retailers are steadily learning the value of reaching out to their customers via seminars, informational products, and more. If you use those same tools to approach them — the same tools you'll find outlined in the remainder of this book! — they'll respond surprisingly well.

The trick is to remember that this is a marathon, not a sprint. You will not suddenly convert all of your retailers into fanatically loyal buyers the day you send out an informative e-zine. Instead, positioning yourself as the vendor of choice requires a commitment to an ongoing campaign of education and support. You want your retailers to view you as a partner, and that type of relationship requires both time and effort.

Don't despair. It's never too late to start — and the results are well worth it!

"I wish we could"
are the best words to use
when customers make
unreasonable requests.

The Five Key Points You Need to Know

Point Number One: Become the Vendor of Choice
Let's first look at human nature and consider the things that attract us to certain people. Then let's go beyond that to the point of becoming a trusted resource.

Point Number Two: Think Like a Retailer Think about what's important to every retailer and how you can fill that gap.

Point Number Three: Become the Bottom-line Resource
This should be the goal of every vendor. Why? Because you're saying, "Not everything is going to sell, but we will make sure you always make money with us." Retailers stick with a vendor like that.

Point Number Four: Stand out from the Pack This is much easier than you realize, because most of your competition is still selling the old way. Write down all the things you do for a retailer and distribute that to your retailers. Then wait for the WOWs.

Point Number Five: Make Your Retailers Believe in You
Testimonials. It's called social proof. You can tell retailers how great your products and company are, but they trust it a lot more when their colleagues tell them.

How can I apply what I've learned?

CHAPTER TWO

Education

As the world becomes more complex
the ability to educate your accounts
becomes the fast track to loyalty and success.
— Rick Segel —

☞ What the Retailer Knows

Education is what separates the great retailers from the average retailer and the average retailer from the not-so-great retailer. With an ever-evolving marketplace, there's a constant need for education. Things are changing more and faster than ever before. No one person can keep up with everything.

Add to that the fact that not all retailers are blessed with an equal degree of business acumen. Some are incredibly sophisticated, while others barely have a grasp on the fundamentals. Many, many independent specialty retailers went into business because they had a genuine passion for what they sell: Avid golfers open golf shops; the town's best cook opens a kitchenware store. Sadly, this enthusiasm doesn't translate into an automatic understanding of how retailing works.

This presents an incredible opportunity to vendors. Providing education to your retailers enhances your relationship with them and helps position you as an expert within your industry. The trend toward educational marketing, where retailers present seminars, classes, and workshops for their customers, translates really well into the vendor-retailer relationship. Vendors who present educational resources for retailers, enabling and equipping them to run their stores with less stress and more profit, will effectively differentiate themselves from the competition. Bear in mind, too, that this education means that retailers will be able to sell more of your product without having to resort to super deep discounts — a situation that's good for both of you.

In this section, we're going to cover how to offer educational opportunities to your retailers, as well as what they'd like to learn about.

☞ Be the Expert

To be of ultimate use to your retailer, you want to be the expert, not only in your product line, but in your category. "Know what the trends are within your category—and how your category is doing in comparison to the rest of the marketplace," says Lori Osborne, an account manager with ConAgra Foods, one of the largest grocery vendors in the country. "This is the type of information that you can share with your retailers that they really can't get anyplace else."

Remember, 99.9 percent of retailers will tell you they're trapped in their store. They can't or don't get out of their place to check out what their competitors are doing. On the other hand, that's what sales reps are doing each and every day. You have access to the type of information they just can't get to!

Sharing industry findings with your retailers is one way to help them improve their understanding of your merchandise—and the better your retailers understand your products, the better they'll be able to sell your products. "I'll bring in other resources," Osborne adds. "Experts in a given category to reinforce what I'm saying. Often this will have more impact and give more value to my retailers than I can alone."

The pharmaceutical industry has done this very well by recruiting physicians to discuss new and existing product offerings. It's a model that works in other industries as well. "Utilize your own people," Osborne recommends. "Look at your staff and see who you have that is best equipped to share information effectively with your retailers."

Another option is to draw from the ranks of retail experts and professional speakers to present this information to your retailers. Working with a third party vendor in this way allows you to offer a rich array of information. For example, RIM, the people who make Blackberry, presented *The Retail Kit for Dummies* to their vendors, along with two teleseminars. It was a complete package their vendors really appreciated.

☞ The Value of Training

"Training has always been the weakest area. I've been in the business world one way or another for over sixty years, and this has always been true," says Frank Epstein, a sales professional with decades of experience in the wine, liquor, and spirits industry. Retailers are often reluctant to train staffers for fear that they'll lose a high-quality employee as soon as a better paying job comes along.

However, this is short sighted. Work with your retailers to understand the value of training. "If you train your people and you give them a good environment to work in, the majority of them will stay," Epstein explains. "There are three reasons that trained people who are pleased with their work situation leave. One: They're lured away by a bigger, better name. Two: They move away from the area. Three: They die. There's not much, really, that you can do about those last two."

☞ Be in the Moment

Maurice Breton, president of Comfort One Shoes, a successful retailer with over 20 stores, relies on his reps to keep retailers up-to-date: "We like to have Saturday morning meetings, with all staff, from all of our stores. We always invite one or two of our key sales reps to discuss the features, benefits, construction, materials, and fit characteristics of their product line.

"As we have our sales associates and store managers there, we feel that these Saturday morning meetings are 'of the moment.' We want him telling about the products that are in the store right now, not something that may or may not come in six months from now."

Tomorrow's possibilities are often more exciting than today's realities, but the truth is that retailers can sell only what they have in their stores RIGHT NOW.

☞ Offer Teleseminars for Your Retailers

A twist on the teleconference is the seminar or workshop that uses a telephone bridge line. Simply by having all of your retailers dial into a phone conference, they can reap the benefits of your educational offerings without ever having to leave their shops.

This is an ideal opportunity to call on a retailing expert to provide these services on your behalf. There are many advantages to this: Your retailers are far more likely to tune in to someone with a little "star power."

You can offer a variety of classes from beginning advertising to more advanced topics, such as managing your buying. Any type of informative seminar or workshop helps you capitalize on the trend of the moment: educational marketing.

Establishing yourself as the expert is the sweet spot in retail today. Customers value a knowledgeable, insightful salesperson to the point where even the omnipresent issue of price ceases to be so important. The same holds true in the vendor-retailer dynamic: If you're the vendor who can provide the extra value to your customers, that will override almost every other concern!

Pick one night a month to hold your classes. Mondays, Tuesdays, or Wednesdays work best. Supply a handout in PDF format that retailers can download from your website and read (or print) no matter what kind of computer they use. Provide room on the handout for the retailer to make notes — there will always be things that come up in discussion that they'll want to remember!

If you record the teleseminars (many providers offer this service for free or a nominal fee), you can then offer the recordings to retailers to use as training tools with their sales staff. Put these recordings on your website, so retailers can download and listen to them at their leisure.

One great way to format your teleseminars is to host a weekly call-in event where retailers can call in and have experts answer their questions. Make no mistake: This is customer service at its finest. You're learning about and addressing customer needs and concerns as they arise.

☞ Webinars

Companies such as Webex and StreamLogic offer vendors the ability to hold meetings online with graphics. Participants call into a bridge line while viewing a graphic presentation online. This graphic presentation can offer streaming video — great if you're doing product demonstrations — or PowerPoint-style slide shows.

As an added bonus, some webinar hosting sites allow participants to "archive" the presentation, so that retailers who were unable to view the presentation at the scheduled time can access it later.

☞ Offer Tutorial Courses– Electronically

Contract with a training professional to create 20-minute presentations on topics of importance, and make these available in audio or video in CD, DVD, or VHS formats. Topics covered could range from the basics of customer service to creating effective promotions to loss prevention techniques — whatever will be of the most interest for your customer base.

Add a workbook containing self-tests so retailers can see how well they are mastering each topic. Make sure to provide the answers in a checklist or other handy format as they might be the only reference guide your retailer has on the subject!

These audio or video presentations could be given away as an incentive or a bonus item, such as for placing an order or visiting your booth at a tradeshow. You can also sell the presentations as a training tool.

Consider creating training videos and distributing them to your retailers. Having your company sponsor the training videos that retailers use to train their new employees, or further enhance the skills of their existing employees, is a great way to strengthen your relationship with your retailers and position your organization as the expert in the field.

☞ Creative Clipping

Contract with a clipping bureau to collect copies of ads from other retailers. Clipping services also provide composite reports of the print ads within a particular industry.

Add your commentary about the ads — what works, what doesn't — and forward the ads to your accounts. This will assist your retailers by showing them how other businesses are advertising, as well as giving some insight into effective strategies. You may help your retailers avoid making some common mistakes, simply by pointing out where other retailers go wrong!

☞ Offer Suggestion Books for Displays

The more information you can offer your retailers the better. Equip your sales representatives with booklets that suggest ways of displaying your merchandise. Include photos and step-by-step guides so retailers can see how to mount these displays.

Remember to update these booklets frequently. Did you have crowds of complimentary retailers admiring the display at the last tradeshow? Take some pictures and put together a guide telling them how they can recreate the effect in their own stores.

For maximum effect, have this guide available both at the tradeshow and on the road with your reps. That way your entire audience has the option of creating the display themselves!

☞ Reps Are Teachers, Too!

"I really view my role as educational," says Mike Green, one of the leading sales reps for Amesbury Chairs. "If I take the time to teach the sales staff about my product line and the benefits it offers, then it'll be easier for them to sell it. People like to do what's easy, so I make it easy for them."

Offer to have your sales representatives hold after-hours classes for retailers and their staff. Retailers will appreciate your reducing the amount of training they have to provide to all new hires.

Certain skills, such as how retailers can improve their customer service, are more effectively taught face-to-face than by simply saying customer service needs to be improved.

Other skills are more suited for computer-based learning — including skills developed by implementing many of the ideas in this book — thereby reducing travel issues.

To encourage your sales force's participation, offer them financial incentives. To build their confidence so they feel comfortable conducting classes for retailers, offer them train-the-trainer seminars from professionals.

☞ Create an Academy

For the ultimate in retailer education, you'll want to look at Steve Lang and his Mon Cheri Academy. Every year, Mon Cheri, one of the leading manufacturers of bridal and special occasion gowns, hosts an intensive series of workshops, seminars, and roundtable discussions for their retailers in a destination city.

"We don't make a penny off of this, not a penny," he explains. "But that's okay. That's not the point. I start from the premise that the vendor's responsibility is not just to make products and services. When IBM was in trouble, they realized that they weren't in the business of selling computers; they were in the business of selling solutions. It transformed their company and saved it from disaster.

"The same is true for any industry," adds Lang. "In the bridal industry, we're selling service and emotion. That's why education is so important. We educate the retailer, so they in turn can educate the ultimate customer, who walks in looking for the dress of her dreams."

The Mon Cheri educational program is all-encompassing, covering selling techniques, store layout, product selection, basic business finances, and more. "The more our retailers know, the more successful they'll be," says Lang. "And the more successful they are, the more successful we'll be.

"You have to really believe in this in order to make it work," he adds. "The programs we do have been imitated but never copied, because people didn't have their hearts in it. You can't do this trying to make a buck or as a sales shtick. Retailers are smart. They'll see right through that. They'll know if you're genuine."

☞ Using Surveys as an Educational Tool

As a manufacturer, distributor, or wholesaler, you are in a unique position to poll your retailers' opinions and experiences—from a simple "How's business?" to the specific "What percentage of your sales do you spend on advertising or payroll?"

The enticement to respond to a survey is that the retailer gets a detailed report on the results. All retailers want to know how their neighbors are doing and how they stack up in comparison.

Surveys can be taken via e-mail, mail, fax, or telephone. Many vendors have built businesses by getting a reputation for conducting annual surveys that provide valuable results to the retailer.

Let's not overlook the value of this information to you, as well. The information gathered has real value. You can create reports using this data and submit it to the press, both general and trade. This has the result of positioning you as the authority within your industry. You become the "go to" vendor—the vendor of choice.

☞ A Different Kind of Survey– Advertising Costs

Instead of surveying retailers, you can do as some companies do for their customers: Research the cost of resources that you'd like to encourage your retailers to use.

For example, you could conduct a survey of advertising costs. How much does it cost to run a television spot on Station X or a half-page print ad in Magazine Y? Our experience tells us that many retailers shy away from different advertising methods because they don't know what the costs are—and not knowing, make false assumptions. Most retailers simply don't have the time to do the legwork and investigate the truth of what they already "know."

Ideally, what you're looking to create is a series of benchmarks. Tell your retailers what they should expect to spend for good advertising, better advertising, and the best advertising. To help them have more realistic expectations about how much advertising costs, don't be afraid to split these results up by marketplace. One section can cover large, metropolitan markets (where costs are generally much higher!) and smaller, more rural markets.

Conducting this type of informative survey can provide your retailers with an approximate range of prices for graphic designers, ad agencies, newspaper advertising, magazine advertising, radio spots, and TV commercials. This knowledge can play a pivotal role in helping overcome a retailer's hesitation to try a new media.

Gathering this information is not as difficult as you might think. Every professional association polls its members on similar questions. You might find the information by simply researching the Internet and requesting permission to use the findings.

☞ Share the Success Stories

Retailers want to know what works and what doesn't work. Many retailers aren't as tech-savvy as they might be, and have a hard time ferreting out successful models they can copy, especially when it comes to e-commerce.

Retailers will beat a path to your door if you discover and collect these models from your retail accounts and share them with other retailers. There's nothing in the world as interesting as how the other guy does it!

Collect these success stories in a special section of your website. Include them in your newsletter, both printed and electronic. Share them with your sales reps and encourage them to share the models with their retailers.

This kind of knowledge will make you a resource for your retailers and establish you as a guide to success.

☞ Easy Education – Turn out Tip Booklets

Tip booklets are small books, easy to create and use. They should be filled with facts and useful information, not padded with fluff or sales lingo.

One of the neat things that has happened due to advances in technology is that printing just doesn't cost as much as it used to. Yet fewer and fewer people are using print for marketing purposes. Consider embracing print for your tip booklets to make them stand out as distinctive, powerful tools.

Tip books can be created to cover any aspect of retail business management, such as advertising, store layout, display, personnel, and staff meetings. If you have an area that you've identified as a particular weakness among your retailers, consider creating a tip booklet on that subject.

Tip booklets are typically not more than 20 pages long, and measure 5-1/2" by 8-1/2". Another trend in publishing is toward the tall and narrow pocket-sized booklet, 8-1/2" by 3-3/4".

☞ Become the Source for Information

Use your website as a one-stop source or clearinghouse for retailing information. Load it up with downloadable e-books, special reports, and more. If you can, package this information in several formats: Some retailers learn best by listening to the information, so for them, provide podcasts. Others prefer to watch educational material, so opt for embedded video clips.

For an example of what this might look like, visit www.ricksegel.com and check out the home page. You can download a free e-book right there. As of this writing, it's *The 5,000 Best Sales & Promotion Names Ever Collected!*

---

*Your most unhappy customers
are your greatest source of learning*
— Bill Gates —

The Five Key Points You Need to Know

Point Number One: Be in the Moment Every time
you present educational material to your retailers,
ask yourself: Will this help them RIGHT NOW?
Provide information, tools, and resources they
can use immediately — if not even sooner!

Point Number Two: Knowledge Is Power The best
thing you can do for your retailers is to provide
them with education. They need information
to help them run their stores better, generate
more business, motivate their people, advertise
effectively, and more.

Point Number Three: Learn from Your Retailers
Constantly be on the lookout for great ideas from
the retailers you serve. The rest of your clientele
can learn from the best!

Point Number Four: Embrace Technology Teleseminars,
webinars, online tutorials, and other web-based tools
make connecting with your retailers easier than ever
before.

Point Number Five: Search out Surveys Use surveys
to discover your retailers' common costs and
challenges, and create a sense of benchmarks that
individual storeowners can compare themselves to.

How can I apply what I've learned?

CHAPTER THREE

Topics to Cover

*It's time we focus on ways
to increase our margins by 20%
instead of looking for ways
to reduce our margins by 20%.*

— Rick Segel —

We've spent a little time talking about HOW to offer educational programming to your retailers. Let's take some time here to talk about WHAT to teach them.

Information about the following topics can serve as content for your website, newsletter, and e-zine. You can use these topics to create blog posts or as fodder for daily reminder e-mails.

Finally, you can use this material to create tip booklets. Tip booklets are the fastest and easiest way to position yourself as the concerned partner and resource for your retailers.

☞ Networking

Retailers spend most of the day, every day, dealing with the public. You'd think that they'd have people skills better than almost anyone else — and you'd be right.

However, there are some exceptions. Retailers seldom, if ever, get the chance to get together with their peers. They may run into some colleagues at the annual tradeshow, but that's about it. As a result, many retailers feel that they're remarkably weak in the networking area, and feel self-conscious and out of place at networking events.

This is a shame. Networking can offer retailers many valuable opportunities to promote their stores and form alliances with affiliated businesses that could result in increased sales.

Consider offering instruction on the basics of networking, including what is expected behavior at a networking event and some tried and true networking strategies. It's the type of information your retailers can use time and time again, in a variety of situations, and profit from it every time.

☞ Negotiating Ad Rates

Your retailers might be comfortable negotiating discounts with your sales reps, but the same is not necessarily true when it comes to advertising. Why? Simple. When the retailer is negotiating with advertising venues, they're without the tools they have when they negotiate with you. They don't know the advertising world the way they know their own store. They don't have the background knowledge to inform them when they're getting a good deal and when they could reasonably ask for a better price.

You can remedy this by having one of your staffers do some research or hiring an advertising professional to write a tip book that tells how to negotiate with newspapers, magazines, radio and TV stations, and online advertising venues.

Include the highlights of interviews with sales managers and salespeople from the different media talking about the best ways to get the best deals, and include examples.

☞ Image Advertising vs. Price Advertising

The debate about price advertising versus image advertising has been going on since the dawn of time. However, that doesn't mean it's not all new to your retailers.

Create a booklet that explains each type of advertising. Spell out the rationale behind each one, complete with industry examples if possible. This is an excellent opportunity to demonstrate how products in your category are advertised, and offer retailers options when choosing to promote your merchandise.

☞ Billboards

As you'll read a little later on, billboards are one of the most powerful advertising tools going, whether they're used by vendors or by retailers. Yet these powerful signs are seldom understood, especially by smaller retailers.

Billboards build brands, and successful brands build businesses. Teaching retailers how to use a billboard effectively can help them break out of the "constant sale" mentality. Instead, they'll embrace a more balanced— and profitable—approach to promotion.

Developing a tip booklet—or even a book!—on this topic is easy, because suppliers of billboards are more than happy to co-sponsor books of this nature and will supply you with all of the information you need.

☞ Building the Trust Customer

The trust customer is the buyer who is willing to spend more money for an item because he or she has developed trust in the retailer. These customers pay a premium for the relationship they have with the retailer—and do so with a smile.

More than one store has built their entire business around this type of customer. They work at building relationships and developing that crucial trust element.

As a result, they don't have to focus on lowering prices by 20 percent. They can raise their prices by 20 percent, an obviously more profitable position.

You can create a tip booklet centering on building the Trust Customer. Explain the ways that successful retailers can build trust with their customers. Illustrate with examples of advertising, and spell out exactly how these retailers build their brand.

☞ Low- and No-Cost Advertising Methods

Newspaper, radio, TV, and other forms of advertising are not the retailer's only options for drawing customers. That's great, because those options can be pricey!

There are low and no cost ideas out there that retailers can use to boost traffic.

For example, getting a new customer into the store for the first time is a very expensive proposition. Getting existing customers to come back, for a specific reason, is far more cost-effective.

☞ Merchandise Compatibility

Retailers are often guilty of carrying high-quality product lines in one part of their business, yet lower quality items when it comes to accessories. Great brands have died in good stores because they did not have a good supporting cast.

Rest assured that retailers aren't doing this on purpose. Often, they are unaware of the importance of accessory items or aren't well enough versed in the category to select appropriate accessory items. You can help the retailer and yourself by providing appropriate education.

A useful way to approach this is by producing a simple four-page brochure highlighting other product lines that perform well together with your brand. If you want your merchandise to do better on the selling floor, provide the retailer with the details about other lines that complement yours.

☞ Cable Television Techniques

Good concepts in cable TV advertising are worth a fortune. Unfortunately, many independent retailers aren't aware of them. They find themselves relying upon the expertise of the local cable company, which can be very limited.

To help your retailers use cable TV effectively, find the stores that use this medium most successfully and ask for a copy of their commercials on tape. You'll find that they are usually more than willing to share.

Collect all the dos and don'ts about cable advertising in the format of a tip book. Also, create a video library of cable TV ads that could be compiled into one long-laying presentation of ads, accompanied by a separate worksheet that gives a thumbnail description of the purpose of the ad and its track record.

☞ Cash Flow Management

Cash flow management is an art and a science—and sadly, one that many retailers struggle with. It's far too easy for a business to become overextended, often with tragic results.

If you offer dating terms of payments, assist the retailer in understanding exactly what that means and how this will impact their cash flow. This will help your retailers from becoming trapped in the buy now/sell The Five Key Points you need To Know later/pay much later syndrome. Generally, retailers don't get into trouble because they buy too much merchandise. They get into trouble because they don't KNOW that they've overbought. They don't have the numbers balanced. Sinking too much into inventory leaves inadequate resources to cover expenses. Before you know it, your retailer is in trouble.

Cut the problem off at the pass by introducing your retailers to a simple way to keep track of their buying, such as my Open to Thrive System (see p. 165). Make it easy to understand and use, and your retailers will embrace it. A retailer with a healthy bottom line is a retailer who can continue to buy from you!

☞ Elements of a Winning Promotion

Give your retailers a tool to help them drive traffic and generate sales — often without dropping prices.

Develop a checklist of all the elements needed to create a winning promotion. This can be as simple as a small brochure or as ambitious as a multi-page checklist that includes a detailed explanation of what each element represents.

*If it rains lemons
make lemonade.*

The Five Key Points You Need to Know

Point Number One: Make Education Appealing Focus on offering information your retailers want to know about! Ideally, this is information they can start using NOW to make their business better TODAY!

Point Number Two: Focus on Helping Retailers Connect Teach the basics of networking, including what is expected behavior at a networking event and some tried and true networking strategies.

Point Number Three: No One Understands Advertising Your retailers have a great hunger to better understand advertising. Provide information on negotiating ad rates, the types of advertising, and how to reach out to different types of customers.

Point Number Four: Provide Promotional Support Teach your retailers how to generate more traffic and drive sales, without dropping prices. Make sure you include ways to use signage to build a brand.

Point Number Five: Always Offer More Advise retailers about accessory and complementary products that will help your merchandise sell better.

How can I apply what I've learned?

CHAPTER FOUR

Advertising

---

*Iteration and reiteration
conveys an alien thought
upon a reluctant mind.*
— Source Unknown —

☞ What the Retailer Knows

Advertising is an art and a science. It's also incredibly expensive, and retailers are under constant, intense pressure to buy, buy, buy. It's difficult for many retailers to determine what advertising works, how they can best spend their limited advertising budget, or how to determine if their advertising campaigns are effective.

In this chapter, we're going to explore unique, innovative tactics you can adopt and adapt to WOW your retailers and make their registers ring. When your retailers do better, you'll do better.

☞ Walk the Walk

Advertising is expensive. For a retailer to commit some of his resources to promoting one of your lines or products, he has to have confidence that your merchandise is strong enough and appealing enough to draw in customers.

It's not a decision they make lightly. It is easier for a retailer to feel confident about a product when he knows that the vendor is equally enthused about it. If a manufacturer is not willing to push a given product, why should the retailer?

Demonstrate your company's belief in the product by spelling out what marketing campaigns are affiliated with the merchandise. Let the retailer know what type of advertising is going to be done. Will there be a television, magazine, or web campaign? The more you do, the more the retailer will be likely to do.

☞ Be a Resource

Some retailers are great at designing ads, while others just don't have the knack. Help everyone out by creating an advertising library that your retailers can search for inspiration.

Do this by collecting ads from your accounts. Ask your retailers how well each ad worked. Make note of the type of store, the advertising vehicle — newspaper, magazines, web, radio, or TV spot — and any factors that the retailer felt contributed to the ad's success or failure.

While it's tempting to just accentuate the positive, make sure to jot down any reasons why an ad didn't work. Often, this information can be extremely valuable. It might prove crucial in allowing other retailers to avoid costly mistakes!

Consider creating a "retailers only" section of your website. Use this area to post the ads and notes so your clients can access them at any time. More than one retailer has designed ads in the middle of the night. Having your library available to them 24/7 just reinforces your value and availability to the retailer.

☞ Offer Images

Good images can create the "next big thing." Strong photography can bring a product out of total obscurity and thrust it into the limelight. They say a picture is worth a thousand words. When it comes to retailing, one good picture can be a thousand sales.

Imagine what a thousand sales would mean to one of your retailers. Imagine what it would mean to all of them.

All manufacturers should make a substantial, consistent effort to provide their retailers with professional-quality, attractive images to be used for advertising purposes. The apparel industry has really done well with this, as has the home improvement industry. The common tie between the two? They provide images that speak directly to the emotional effect their products will have upon the consumer's life.

It's not a picture of a beautiful gown. It's a picture of a smiling bride on the happiest day of her life, who just happens to be wearing a beautiful gown. It's not a picture of an attractive faucet. It's a picture of an attractive faucet in a designer bathroom, spilling refreshing water into a spa-like tub, evoking pure rest, relaxation, and luxury.

Create a library of high-quality images. You want the type of work that can be used in national campaigns — retailers and those in the know can tell the difference between professional work and the budget-rate job. Every dime you spend on images will pay for itself ten times over in sales and retailer loyalty.

☞ Create Ads Your Retailers Can Use

Retailers and customers have become increasingly media savvy. One glance at an ad can tell them if the company being portrayed is one to take seriously or just some amateur floundering around where the big boys play. Help your retailers shine by providing them with ads they can use.

This is an idea that has been around for years. However, if you're going to do this, invest in the services of a good graphic designer who understands your industry. There's nothing worse than an ad that's dated — and there's a million subtle things like composition, color, and font choice that can make your ad appear behind the times.

Provide fresh, up-to-date ads. Change them regularly. The public's attention span is short. If they see the same ad too many times, they no longer see it at all.

Additionally, manufacturers' ads traditionally don't do much in the way of promoting the retailer. Remember, you need your retailer to succeed if you're going to do well. Ads you create for your retailers must be store-focused, with the ability to feature the business as well as the benefits of the product.

Give your retailers some flexibility to use the ads. They know their marketplace and can make the subtle adjustments needed to speak to their target audience while still effectively promoting their store — and your products!

☞ Be the Source – Supply Photos and Logos

A great format for cable TV advertising is a store's presentation of a series of photos that changes every six seconds, with a musical background and a voiceover. But photos are expensive for an individual retailer to produce, whereas most manufacturers already have files of high-quality photos, which enable the retailer to meet cable TV's required production quality.

Photos and logos can also be used for a store's website, magazine ads, brochures, direct mail pieces, and of course, newspaper ads. Supplying these resources costs you, the manufacturer or vendor, very little.

Make the photos available as both low- and high-resolution downloads in a section of your website. Retailers will appreciate this service and will prefer buying from you simply because you are supplying the photos. You gain a competitive advantage with very little work.

☞ Cut Through the Red Tape – Offer Retailer-Friendly Co-op Advertising

Co-op advertising has been around for years, but the biggest problem for retailers is filling out the forms and meeting all the requirements to get co-op money. After that's done, they have to wait a long time to get a check. Most retailers feel as if it's not worth the effort.

If you want an effective co-op ad program that is used, streamline the process. Allow a retailer to apply for co-op fund reimbursement without requiring advance approval. Fast track the procedure by making the approval process take only one day, or even better, three hours.

Allow the retailer to fax or e-mail you a copy of the ad with a simple form stating costs and placement, and then issue an immediate credit against any existing invoices.

Some vendors prefer issuing credit while others prefer checks. Still others give checkbooks to their sales reps to speed up the process even more!

☞ Promote Store-Focused Co-op Advertising

Retailers are far more likely to participate in co-op advertising when they perceive a clear benefit to their store. To help build both the store's business and your own, allow the retailer's name to be the most prominent name appearing in the ads.

Too often a vendor's co-op restrictions wind up creating an ad that resembles a dealer-listing ad. Remember that the retailer pays a substantial part of the advertising cost—they're going to want more than a dealer listing ad for their investment. You want the consumer to go to that particular store to look for the merchandise—not just any store.

If retailers cannot reap the benefits of their own ads, they are going to stop participating in your co-op program.

☞ And the Winner Is – Your Annual Advertising Contest

Sponsor an advertising competition that encourages retailers to advertise your products. While these ad competitions drive sales, they also generate great ideas that you can use in becoming a valued resource.

People are motivated by competition. You don't have to look any closer than the television to see the concept in action: From American Idol to Survivor to So You Think You Can Dance, we're enthralled by competition. Everyone wants to be a contestant! Create a competition and you'll bring your most competitive retailers out of the woodwork. The greater the reward, the more participation you'll have – retailers are busy people. You have to make the effort worth their while!

As an added bonus, most retailers enjoy saying they have "award-winning" advertising.

Judge the ads on originality of concept, construction of ad, and any other considerations you deem important.

To have a great advertising contest:

- Make it easy for retailers to enter.

- Categorize entries by size of the store so the smaller stores have a chance at winning in their size category.

- Make the prize worth the effort. You want to give a significant cash prize, but you also want to award a nice plaque or trophy for the store to display for its customers to see.

- Create a strong public relations initiative, with press releases submitted to trade publications. Some vendors advertise pictures of the winners with their trophies or checks.

Creating a great contest is so much easier now because of the web. Much of the time and effort that used to have to go into administering contests can be minimized by use of web resources. Additionally, the easy access to the web puts all of your retailers on a more equal footing: Your smaller stores can compete just as effectively as a larger store.

☞ What a Way to Get Ideas – Have a Sale Competition

Competition doesn't have to be limited to advertising. Ideas for sales and promotions are just as valuable.

The biggest problem in retailing is that most retailers don't know how to run a sale properly. They don't know what goes into designing an effective promotion, nor how to capitalize on the opportunities a great sale offers.

That is why you want to look not only for great sales ideas but also for effective procedures and timing. The more details you can gather about a successful sale, the more valuable this information becomes. In addition to requesting samples of the ads, have your entry requirements ask about store layout, signage, staffing, employee and customer contests, themes, employee meetings, sales performance, and advertising.

☞ The Winner Again – Celebrate Interior Advertising with a Sign Competition

Great signage has built many retail businesses. Some retailers have built entire businesses around effective signage and billboards. Small wonder: Signage is one of the most powerful forms of interior advertising.

Clever phrases get customers talking about a business, and that becomes word-of-mouth advertising—the best form of advertising there is. Customers tell their friends about the funny signs they saw, and before you know it, those friends come in to check things out for themselves.

☞ Share What You Learned

No matter what type of competition you hold, make sure you realize the full benefit of it. The winner and the top contestants have handed you a valuable resource: stunning examples of work your other retailers can emulate!

The value to you of any type of contest is the chance to share the winning ideas with other retailers of your products. You acknowledge the winners, of course, and "raise the bar" in your industry.

Print either the winning concepts or all the entries in a book or booklet to give away to all of your retailers. The number of entries will determine the size of what you publish and how often you choose to publish it.

☞ Supply the Signage

It's easy to give ideas for signage, but supplying good signs always helps sell merchandise.

This idea has been around for years, but you can put a different twist on it by furnishing creative tips on how to use the signs, where to put them, and what kind of positive effect the signage could have on the store's business.

Develop signs with enough flexibility to incorporate the store's logo as well as your own.

☞ It's All About Ideas – Offer Sign Concepts

The easiest ways to become a sign resource for your retailers is to devote a section of your website to professionally designed store signs. Make sure that retailers can download full-sized signs. The retailer can then have the signs printed.

An interesting twist is to allow the retailers to sketch a sign, fax or e-mail it to you, and have your graphic designer recreate it in a PDF file that the retailer can download and bring to her printer.

Again, you're taking advantage of technology to make life easy for your retailer. All your store owner has to do is forward the file to her printer, and they take care of the rest!

☞ Offer Ad Coaching

You can have the best advertising ideas in the world, but they're no good to anybody if your retailers don't use them. Getting people to act on new initiatives can be tricky.

Coaching is growing in popularity in all aspects of business. Consider offering a service, for a minimal fee, whereby an advertising coach talks to the retailer for 30 minutes on a weekly basis. The purpose of each coaching session is to ensure that the ideas the retailer likes are acted on—the friendly reminder we all need at times.

Coaches don't have to be advertising or design specialists as long as they are understanding individuals with a basic comprehension of marketing and what the retailer is trying to accomplish. The growing popularity of coaching has increased the number and types of coaches available today. A web search will uncover an abundance of qualified coaches that you can work with, a far less expensive method than the use of internal personnel.

If you really want to offer your retailers the ultimate in ad coaching, bring in a retail expert to consult with your customers regularly. This can be as simple as arranging a two-hour call-in session once a week, where your clientele can connect directly with the best!

☞ Offer a Monthly Advertising Service That Provides Ads

This is a service in which you send retailers advertising ideas, copy, concepts, and actual ads. The most cost efficient way of doing so today is via your website, but e-mail and old-fashioned mail work just fine.

Include ad ideas from other industries. An easy way to do this is to create a separate e-zine specifically filled with these ads and the copy and concepts that support them, and send it out to every retailer on your list once or twice a month.

There is some controversy about whether manufacturers should charge for this type of service. While it is impressive to provide resources for free, it's also important to note that the majority of people don't value what they don't pay for. You could safely charge a fee for a service like this. Remember the old saying "He who gives freely gives twice"!

☞ Create an Advertising E-zine

Send your retailers a weekly e-mail of helpful tips, tools, and resources about retail advertising. These e-mails don't have to be lengthy. In fact, they are more effective when they are short and to the point.

For example, one week you could highlight one of the most powerful types of ads: the Q & A ad. You could give an example of a Q & A ad, give a template for retailers to create their own ad, explain why this type of ad is so powerful, and share a success story from a retailer who used Q & A ads to build her business.

The weekly contact puts your company name in front of your customers even if they don't use any of the ideas.

Just the fact that you are offering the ideas goes a long way toward keeping you in the mind of each retailer.

☞ Best Business-building Ad – Offer a "Q&A" Ad Service

The question and answer ad format is one of the most successful advertising concepts ever created. It is used successfully by many different types of retailers over a long term.

Let's first define the Q&A ad. It is a series of single column, 4-inch-long ads that run in local newspapers once a week, 52 weeks a year. The headline remains consistent (e.g., "Ask the Gift Expert," or whatever subject you are the expert about). A small picture or caricature sketch of the owner or manager of the retail business is included, along with his or her name and a title, such as giftware expert or professional. A short question is followed by an answer. At the bottom of the ad is the store logo.

Where you, the manufacturer, play a part is to introduce the concept to one retailer in each media market and help develop the questions and answers. This type of advertising builds your retailer's brand (as well as your own) and positions each retailer as the expert. It also positions your company as an authority in your industry. You become the source for the retailing experts.

☞ Keep Them Advertising – The Power of the Ad Budget

Getting retailers to budget for their advertising spending is one of the most challenging jobs for any consultant. Whatever help you can offer will go a long way toward establishing you with your retailers.

You can accomplish this educational task in several ways: by producing an informative booklet, creating a section on your website, setting up a teleconference, or organizing a live seminar.

Make sure your programming includes these benefits of ad budgeting:

- Retailers save money by negotiating more favorable media rates for total yearly expenditures rather than for short-term spurts.

- Retailers increase their name recognition from the proven repetitions that a long-term commitment to advertising makes possible.

- Retailers streamline their buying patterns, since long-term advertising focuses them on the merchandise needed to back up a long-term ad campaign.

☞ Host an Advertising Hotline

An advertising hotline is exactly what it sounds like: a 1-800 number for your retailers to call for advice and answers to their advertising questions. Enhance this idea by inviting retailers to send you a video tape or file, audio tape or file, or copies of their ads and supporting materials and having one of your staff assist the retailer in resolving problems. A retailer could also forward a media contract before signing it so a staff person could check the contract rate against established media guides.

This kind of service does not require internal staffing; it can be outsourced for a more cost-efficient result. There are companies that specialize in providing this kind of one-on-one coaching.

However, it is essential that you promote this service to your retailers. They will realize the benefit of the hotline only if they call it!

☞ Offer a Proofing Service for Ads

Invite retailers to send an ad proof to one of your eagle-eyed staffers so it can be reviewed quickly for accuracy and completeness before the retailer approves its release to the media. Sometimes a set of fresh eyes will see errors that would otherwise be missed — until it's too late!

☞ Be the Expert – Have a Sales Event Helpline

Running a sale event is a specialized skill that requires professional expertise. The problem is that professionals can be expensive, which almost defeats the purpose of running the sale. Having a helpline to assist your retailers run sales can pay huge dividends.

If you don't have someone capable of providing such advice, subcontract the work to an expert who will return calls to retailers within 12 hours. A sales event helpline is a wonderful service that retailers will greatly appreciate.

☞ Let's Get Together – Create a Retail Advertising Advisory Panel

Ask a select group of blue-ribbon retailers, key salespeople, marketing personnel, and production people to meet once a year to discuss issues of advertising. The panel's agenda should include issues and trends that affect the industry, retailers, manufacturing, and wholesaling.

Such meetings generally take place at a tradeshow,but you could also schedule meetings at other times. Consider having web meetings or teleconferences throughout the year. Publish results in company newsletters. The goal for a program such as this is to increase the efficiency of everyone's advertising investments.

Make sure you have an advertising professional on your retail advisory panel. This person's job is to ensure that when the ideas start flying around, they are actually doable. Try to have someone from your ad department on the panel, but if you can attract an advertising pro who doesn't work for you to attend these meetings, even better. An outside voice brings no preconceived beliefs to say, "That was tried before and it didn't work."

For best results, have your advisory panel facilitated by someone who knows how to direct a meeting, keep it running, and see that everybody contributes, not just a few dominant voices. The facilitator should have an agenda and make sure the meeting stays on task and on time. These sessions should be recorded and transcribed at a later time.

☞ Plan, Plan, Plan – Create an Advertising Workbook

Retailers too often place their advertising week to week. If you develop a workbook, you can assist the retailer in planning ads for the quarters of the year (and budgeting accordingly)!

The workbook is a great place to offer seasonal ideas for ads and promotions.

Put the workbook and a budget planning device online, so that the retailer can access it easily. Use a common format, such as Excel or other spreadsheet program, which allows retailers to input their last 12-month sales history or future sales goals.

Have the budget planning device ask what percentage of their sales they want to allocate to advertising and what media they want to use. Individual retailers could maintain their information securely on your website if you make each record password-protected.

Again, this is a project you could design in-house. However, it might be far more efficient and cost-effective if you bring in a consultant to handle the job.

☞ A Little Incentive – Pay Retailers for Advertising Results

Offer an incentive in the form of credit or cash to retailers who furnish you with an advertising response report. Have them include a copy of the ad with a form that addresses these factors:

- Info about how the ad pulled
- Pictures of how the merchandise was displayed

- Examples of signage

- Sell-through

- Weather and any community activities taking place during the run of the ad

- Interesting anecdotes

You must ask the retailers if they want this information shared with others. Some will be glad to share while others will want the name of their store withheld.

A little incentive goes a long way. You can get great information very easily this way.

☞ Success Sells–Share Advertising Success Stories

Use a printed newsletter, online newsletter, or e-zine to tell retailers about the successes others have had advertising your merchandise. Include photos, testimonials, and stories of unique experiences with customers. Testimonials and referrals are the best form of advertising, and this sharing concept encourages more of it.

☞ Develop a Postcard Reminder Service

Retailers are busier than ever, so save their time by reaching them with a short message: the postcard. Used in a series, postcards can remind retailers of your advertising resources, toll-free helpline, an upcoming conference or tradeshow, or a series of helpful hints on how to improve their business.

☞ Be Creative – Reward Sales Reps for Orders with Ad Plans

Stores that advertise your product will sell more of it. So focus the retailer on advertising your product and enjoy a win/win for everyone.

Create a bonus for your sales reps who write orders that have ad plans attached. Further reward those reps who follow through, with bonuses paid only on the completion of the plan.

To be eligible, a sales rep's order should be accompanied by an advertising plan, display plan, signage plan, and a request for any necessary support material from the manufacturer.

☞ Make It Easy to Show Your Stuff – Supply Display Props

Mannequins, backdrops, build-ups, lamps, illuminated signage, and other display props are great ways to cement in the customer's mind the branding of both the retail store and your products, especially when the props you supply already bear your logo, company name, or other identifiers.

☞ It's Worked for Years – Exterior Signage

Everyone remembers the Coca-Cola signs of years ago that hung over small storefronts. Today, many small retailers on a budget will allow you to do the same thing: co-brand with them for the signage that appears outside their building or on the signboard at a shopping center.

☞ Make Them a Star – Feature a Retailer in Your Advertising

When you advertise your products in trade magazines, feature one of your better retailers giving a testimonial about the profitability and sell-through of your products. Be sure the ad profiles the retailer. Frame a copy of the ad and deliver it to the retailer.

The behavior that is rewarded is the behavior that is repeated.

— Rick Segel —

The Five Key Points You Need to Know

Point Number One: Walk the Walk If you want your retailers to support and promote your products, your organization has to be willing to support and promote your products! Position yourself as the go-to resource your retailers can turn to for guidance, support, and advertising materials.

Point Number Two: Do the Groundwork Provide the ads, images, logos, copy, and collateral materials your retailers can use to advertise their store and your brand. Make it easy for your retailers and they'll participate.

Point Number Three: Use Competitions to Grow Sponsor an advertising competition that encourages retailers to advertise your products. While these ad competitions drive sales, they also generate great ideas that you can use in becoming a valued resource. Or have your retailers compete to have the best sale, the best signs — you name it.

Point Number Four: Support Signage Signage is one of the most powerful and underutilized tools in retail today. Many store owners don't understand how effective signs can be. Make a concerted effort to promote sign usage among your retailers.

Point Number Five: Leverage the Logistics Make it easy for your retailers to advertise effectively by helping them handle the nuts and bolts: proofing the ads, providing coaching to guide the ad creation process, helping design and run sales events, and more.

How can I apply what I've learned?

CHAPTER FIVE

Promotions

All Business is Show Business.

☞ What the Retailer Knows

There are many times when retailers want to generate traffic, yet might not want to have a sale. Having too many sales can negatively affect a store's reputation, especially if it's a high-end or boutique retailer. That's when promotions become critical.

At the same time, as our culture transforms shopping from a necessity into a form of entertainment, unique, effective promotions can help retailers position themselves as a fun destination. If you can help the retailer plan and implement these promotions, you're well on your way to becoming the vendor of choice!

In this chapter, we'll be focusing on non-sale price promotions that can spotlight, focus, and bring lots of attention to your retailers' businesses.

☞ Promotion Doesn't Mean Sale

We're going to hit this first and foremost, because it's important. Promotions DO NOT have to represent price reductions. In fact, as shopping has evolved from a necessity to a form of entertainment, the role of promotions has changed.

Manufacturers should change their focus from price to the excitement and buzz that can be generated by a good promotion. For an example, let's take a look at the movie industry.

Everybody's favorite boy wizard, Harry Potter, can generate tremendous excitement at the box office. The first Harry Potter film generated over $400 million in revenue in two weeks, although the whole world knew that the film could soon be seen on a $3 video rental.

People still flocked to the theaters. Why? They could have saved over 90 percent, but financial considerations were not what motivated their decisions. Instead, people paid full price to be part of the buzz and excitement generated by all the hoopla.

The same could happen at your retailers' stores. The key is finding the promotion that excites enough shoppers and generates tremendous word of mouth.

☞ Use a Book as a Promotional Offer

If you use any direct mail and you are looking for an immediate response from retailers, include an offer that they can't resist. Make this offer time-sensitive — to collect the promotional offer, they must respond by the expiration date.

A promotion used very successfully by many vendors is the offer of a free book. Books are relatively inexpensive to produce and create an impression of great value, which is why offers of free books consistently generate high response rates. In fact, my book *The Retail Kit for Dummies* has been used many times in just this way.

☞ Teleconference to the Top

The primary purpose of communications technology is to connect people. Why not use a teleconference to connect your retailers with the people who can help them the most? Arrange a teleconference where your stores can talk to the president of your company, your designers, sales managers, and advertising executives on a quarterly or semiannual basis. Use teleconferencing!

Announce each teleconference by sending your retailers a postcard, and have your sales reps and customer service departments remind them of the upcoming event.

This concept is very successful and is now commonplace on Wall Street, where analysts are invited to a quarterly financial review and allowed to ask questions. This is an ideal way to discuss promotional ideas and spark creative thinking. There's an even better benefit: You're helping your retailers become more involved with your company, which is vital to building lasting relationships.

☞ Create a Community

"Any time you gather people together to discuss things of interest to them, common problems they all face, you're creating something special. There's a real synergy there, and it's very powerful." So says Steve Lang, owner and president of Mon Cheri. "But you can't always get everyone in the same place at the same time."

Lang created www.bridalsupport.com as a meeting place for retailers in his industry. This website features a discussion board where retailers can post questions, answer questions, and more. Members log on to share great ideas, seek advice, and commiserate over challenges. Back and forth discussion occurs between Lang and his team AND the retailers, but more importantly, among the retailers who participate on the message board.

It's a concept that can work in any industry and is ideal for discussing promotional ideas. Retailers can share what worked for them and what ideas fell flat. It's a powerful tool, and because retailers are constantly congregating in "your yard" it's a subtle yet effective reinforcement of the value of your relationship.

☞ Sharing Hot Tips – Put Success Stories to Work

Maintain a file of advertising success stories so that when you receive an order from a sales rep for a particular item, you can send a postcard or note to that retailer ahead of the order telling of the success of another retailer's advertising or promotion of that item.

You're not only validating the retailer's decision to purchase your merchandise, you're helping them sell it successfully!

☞ Let Them Wear Your Name—An Alternative Outlet for Co-op Dollars

In addition to distributing earned co-op advertising money in traditional ways, offer an online catalog of company logo specialty items that retailers can order at large discounts, such as sweaters, polo shirts, mugs, and hats.

There are two benefits of such a program:

1. The retailer has a way of rewarding staff.

2. The smaller, loyal retailer has an incentive for using co-op advertising at any level.

Though small stores might say they do not want to waste their time doing co-op advertising to collect only $25, they might see greater value in collecting a sweater for a staff person that's worth much more.

☞ Wearing the Vendor's Name— Dressed to Sell

You can offer to your retailers a program whereby their employees can purchase signature clothing directly from the manufacturer. Almost every company today offers some type of shirt for its employees.

Why not expand the idea to offer your retailers clothing to be worn at work for reduced prices — or even free? Signature clothing helps promote your products and makes the staff more aware of your merchandise. It's also a great help for retailers trying to bring some uniformity to what their staff wears.

An added twist is to get your apparel suppliers to offer their merchandise for the retail staff to wear on the sales floor.

Be open to co-branding opportunities: If your retailer carries two or three other powerful but non-competing brands, consider how you could work together to get maximum bang for the buck!

☞ Create an Encyclopedia of Non-Sale Promotions

Position yourself as a resource for your retailers. Start gathering examples of the best promotions that retailers have held to create excitement and sell merchandise without dropping prices.

You can put this encyclopedia on your website in a retailers-only area. Create a page focused solely on non-sale promotions. Make sure each event has a complete description that includes its title, theme, purpose, type of customer attracted, sales increases if any, increases to store's database, personnel required, and expenses. Include as many pictures as possible to help your retailers envision the promotion. You want this to be a complete how-to library of promotional ideas.

Make sure to include tips from the non-sale promotion page through your newsletter. This will raise awareness of the encyclopedia and encourage your retailers to check it out regularly for new ideas.

☞ Encourage Retailers to Submit Promotions

Getting them to share ideas isn't difficult. Incentives can be presented as contests, financial consideration, or just recognition.

Everyone likes to be recognized as an innovative, savvy retailer. Your goal is to gain a reputation of providing a free service of use to retailers.

☞ Community Service Projects

We hear all the time about the global marketplace and how there are no boundaries anymore — yet people still care about their backyards and neighborhoods as passionately as ever before.

Staying involved in community service projects is an integral part of any retailer's marketing effort. Customers want to do business with people who care about their communities and the world around them.

As a vendor, you might offer an award to your retailers for the best community service project. You can do so through state retail associations, many of which recognize retailers with award programs that are vendor-sponsored.

☞ Help Retailers Create an Electronic Newsletter

E-zines are powerful, proven marketing tools, yet many retailers are still struggling to produce and use them. If your company can create and publish a shell for them to use, your company name will be displayed as a sponsor.

This is a constant source of advertising to that retailer's customers for very little money. Additionally, you're reinforcing your position as a valuable resource to that retailer.

Write most of the e-zine for your retailers, and allow them to just plug in a story or ad in the format you created. Again, the easier you make it for your retailers, the more likely they will be to use the e-zine.

One inexpensive way of producing this e-zine is to form a strategic alliance with a company such as Microsoft's Bcentral.com, which publishes electronic newsletters. Be aware that there are also many other smaller vendors who can do just as good a job.

☞ Supply Press Releases for Your Retailers to Use

Instead of sending out a press release about one of your new products or lines — news that would seldom get local coverage — write a press release that features the retailer. This will create that vital element — hometown interest — that local media thrives on.

There are two ways to go about this: You can have your retailers send you a list of local publications they'd like press releases submitted to, or you can send a draft of the release to retailers to further customize it and submit themselves.

Some retailers will prefer to realize the benefit while doing as little work as possible, while others want the control to deal with the local press directly. Knowing your clients is key when deciding how to supply press releases.

☞ Create Press Release Templates

Create a simple template for a press release that retailers can use to easily generate their own press releases. Make it a fill-in-the-blank style, where retailers have to enter only their store name, address, and a short, unique phrase describing the store.

Offer different templates for announcing sales, new products, and new or retiring employees. Consider seasonal- and holiday-themed releases, especially for unusual or off-beat holidays that happen during traditionally slow news times when the media is hungry for news.

Structure your releases to include a line that says "(ABC Retailer), carrying such famous brands as _____" and fill in your brand's name. Make these templates available on your website, and regularly include reminders to send out press releases in your newsletter.

☞ Collect Reasons to Use a Press Release

Creating press releases is only half the battle: Retailers need to know why and when to use press releases. Press releases are a powerful tool, but to be effective, they must be used properly.

Collect reasons why and how your retailers can use press releases. Add in tips on what makes an effective press release, including local interest and a news-worthy angle.

Distribute this information via a section of your website, such as the area where you archive press release templates. This information will also make a great article for your newsletter or e-zine, or you could expand it into a tips booklet.

☞ Provide Page Content to Retailers' Websites

The Internet has become an established part of how retailers do business. Most retailers know that they need a website, but they don't know what they're supposed to put on it or how to realize the maximum benefit from their web presence.

This creates a major opportunity for manufacturers. By helping retailers put together websites or parts of websites, you're providing a real service of value. Most retailers have small websites and don't have the money, time, or knowledge to devote to making the most of the web.

Offer retailers prepared pages that work with their existing sites. This helps the retailer have a more comprehensive, professional-looking, quality site, and the manufacturer gets some inexpensive advertising.

☞ Customer Appreciation Day–Not As Goofy As It Sounds!

Customer Appreciation Day may be the most overworked title in the retailing world, yet it is still surprisingly effective for many different types of retailers and vendors.

These retailers turn Customer Appreciation Day into major events. They ask for vendor participation and host high-profile, heavily publicized festivities. These events can include demonstrations, trunk shows, and free giveaway items, all or some of which could be provided by your company.

These events can result in major traffic and revenue-producing opportunities. Suggest the concept to your accounts. Generally, customer appreciation events create a true party atmosphere and include free refreshments. They have to be fun!

☞ Display Pros to the Rescue

Every retailer is on a constant, never-ending search for a way to display merchandise. Larger stores have the buying power that gets their vendors to provide specialized one-on-one assistance, but it's often the smaller, independent stores that need the help the most.

This is a perfect opportunity for your organization! You already have this expertise!

Share what you and your team know! Reach out to these accounts with display ideas, techniques, workshops, or books of tips. Even photographs go a long way toward gaining your retailers' appreciation. Don't forget the props! A manufacturer's supplying of props (free when possible or at a nominal fee when necessary) is also appreciated.

Some manufacturers work out strategic alliances with various display supply houses to offer group discounts for specific items. This savings will be appreciated by your retailers.

Often, the simplest way is the best: Creating a list of resources where retailers can purchase props and supplies eliminates a lot of legwork on the retailer's part.

☞ Show 'Em How to Show It

Consider offering your retailers the services of a retail display specialist. These skilled professionals have all the skills and know-how to set up a knockout display.

This specialist would travel around to the stores primarily to help the retailer display the manufacturer's merchandise. As a secondary benefit, he or she could offer some assistance with general display issues.

Again, you're reinforcing that your company is interested and invested in helping the retailer succeed. This is a very concrete way of putting your money where your mouth is.

☞ Take It on the Road

Create a road show between your annual or semiannual tradeshows. This tradition comes from the hardware industry, where it has worked effectively for years.

How does it work? The salesperson in the field, the manufacturer's rep or independent salesperson, presents to retailers a small catalog of product offerings that offer combinations of special dating, pricing, and delivery.

This catalog is the "road show" — a great way to get some additional products and items into your account.

It is particularly effective in those industries where tradeshows are few and far between, or in territories where most of your retailers don't attend the markets.

Now consider taking that familiar idea and "twisting" it. Instead of bringing your merchandise out on the road, present your educational offerings that way. Bring retailers together to share in the best display ideas, the best ads, the best product-plus offers.

Do this for free. Think about it: What built the Internet? In large part, the fact that it is full of free content. When your retailers ask about the charge for the event, tell them you simply want them to do well.

☞ Pay Them to Plan

There are two types of retailers: those who know what they're going to be doing five years from now and those who aren't sure what they'll be doing five minutes from now. The first type make your life a little easier, don't they?

Give them a break by offering price incentives to retailers who order seasonally instead of for at-once delivery. Make sure you make this policy well known. It may be a powerful enough incentive to motivate some of your other retailers to consider ordering on a seasonal basis.

☞ The Truckload Sale

Popular among manufacturers of power equipment, the truckload sale concept has begun to creep into the home furnishings and carpeting world. A truckload sale always generates excitement and will bring in surprising amounts of traffic.

To hold a truckload sale, the vendor simply loads up an attractive truck with his merchandise and holds a large sale in the parking lot. Working together with the retailer, it can be a tremendously profitable event, and it saves the retailer from having to order all the items.

Pre-event publicity is critical to the success of a truckload sale, so if you're considering doing this with your retailers, make sure to include pre-sale publicity in your planning. Working with your retailer and perhaps offering some assistance with advertising the event can be well worth your while and will be very appreciated.

☞ The Trunk Show

"If you do a trunk show right, it's absolutely irresistible," says Angelo Marzocchi, a sales professional in the bridal and special occasion wear market. "I have a trunk show every single weekend. It's a great event to introduce a new collection. It allows retailers to bring their buyers together with the latest, greatest, new things before they can get them anywhere else." Marzocchi has discovered that, "the lure of the new is absolutely incredible." Customers follow him from show to show, often driving hundreds of miles across state lines to see the collection.

"They're trunk show groupies," Marzocchi laughs. They're also customers that the retailer had little to no chance of connecting with any other way. A trunk show will bring in customers that your retailer would never ordinarily see.

At a trunk show, the manufacturer brings the merchandise to the retail store. In some cases, customers place orders; in others, customers take their purchases with them. Either way, the retailer pays only for the items ordered or sold, without being responsible for preordering all of the merchandise.

The benefit that the manufacturer provides to the retailer goes far beyond the added traffic and additional customers that come for the trunk sale. Because customers pay for their merchandise before the retailer does, the store both realizes a profit and enjoys free financing.

Key to having an effective trunk show is pre-show promotion. Marzocchi, who sees 40-50 individual customers per show, strongly recommends a strong advertising effort behind the show. "Repetitive ads work really well for this type of event," he says. Another idea is to have themed trunk shows. "We do one for prom season, with all the pomp and ceremony that goes with the prom,"he explains. "We promote it through the schools as well as online, and it goes extremely well."

☞ Keep Them Informed – What's New, What's Up, What's Happening?

"You want to position your company as the category expert," Lori Osborne says. "It's fantastic when your stores know that they can turn to you for information on the latest trends, what changes are happening, and so on."

Use your newsletter or e-zine topical information about what's happening in your industry and with companies that affect your industry. Just because your accounts might be small Mom and Pop stores or midsize retailers doesn't mean they're not intensely interested in what's happening on a larger stage. In fact, smaller stores love to know what is happening at big stores. Feed their hunger to know with healthy helpings of policy changes, gossip, management changes, or retail expansions.

☞ Start a Book Club

"You never stop learning," says Steve Lang of Mon Cheri. "I'm always on the lookout for the next great idea, the next bit of information that will allow me to do business better."

Angelo Marzocchi agrees. "I'm constantly reading motivational books and books that can help me improve."

They're not alone. Most retailers have a strong desire to learn and grow, and appreciate anything you can do to help them in their journey. One way to do this is to start a book club.

Offer retailers books on retail issues. Develop a form for them to sign up for your Book-of-the-Quarter Club and agree to be billed once a quarter. Select the very best books that you can find: ones that will speak to your retailers and their needs. On the cover of each book, stick a self-promotional sticker that identifies you as a vendor of choice.

☞ Who's the Ideal Customer – A Contest That Works for You

An interesting promotional idea that becomes a win/win for both you and your retailer is a contest to find the consumer who represents your product's ideal user.

The idea comes from a promotion called "In Search of the Leslie Fay Woman," conducted by Leslie Fay, a women's dress company. What the company was looking for was its ultimate loyal customer, who loved the merchandise, used it, and was proud to be associated with it.

More recently, the concept has been used with phenomenal success by Dewar's Scotch.

To enter the "In Search of the (Your Product Name) Person" contest, customers visit the store. The promotion works well for a range of products, from hardware to automobiles. It involves the retailer in encouraging its customer to enter. The cost is minimal because the prize winners receive merchandise.

A variation of this ad is to profile someone who is perhaps not your best customer, but your best-known customer.

Other benefits of this promotion are that it helps both the manufacturer and the retailer define who their targeted customers are, and the retailer builds a mailing list for future promotions.

☞ The Packaging Difference

Impress your retailers by the way your merchandise is packaged when it is received at the store. Your professional image will, in turn, impress the ultimate consumer. The smallest things can sometimes have the biggest impact:

- Does the outside of your delivery box indicate quality and professionalism?

- Does the packaging tape have your logo on it?

- Does the box have your company name printed on it?

- When the UPS driver opens the truck, can the retailer immediately distinguish your packages among the hundreds of others?

• Is your image consistent — from the tradeshow experience to the receiving room to the sales floor to the customer's home?

☞ Leave a Paper Trail – Supply Ad Materials

Statement inserts and bag stuffers have been an advertising technique employed by manufacturers for years, and they are still effective promotional tools.

Take the concept a step further by offering retailers a supply of basic capabilities brochures to place in strategic locations. A capabilities brochure is a pamphlet that contains a description and brief history of the store, what the store does, directions to it, type of merchandise carried — featuring yours, of course! — with your company name and a photo of your merchandise. These tri-fold brochures begin with a single piece of 8.5"x11" paper and a template for which the retailer supplies its logo, copy, and photographs.

The benefit of this promotion is that it cements the relationship between the store and the vendor: Retailers continue to carry a line of merchandise that is named in their own brochures.

☞ Seek Out Third Party Endorsements

Third party endorsements of your products can be powerful selling tools for the retailer. Their customers want to drink the wines that Wine Spectator recommends, drive the cars that Motor Trend awards, and wear the clothes that appear on the Top Ten Best Dressed lists.

Courting the consumer media read by your retailer's target audience can pay off handsomely. Sending samples, entering judging competitions, and doing the best you can to create a high profile makes it easier for the retailer to sell your products.

Gild the lily by making sure to send copies of relevant editorial coverage, announcements of prizes won and other third party endorsement products to your retailers. Make this information available via your website and remind your sales reps to bring it up when they're on-site.

☞ The Shop in the Store

Many, many vendors have been successful in creating a shop-within-a-store in major department stores. It's a concept that can transition into smaller independent stores.

Ideally, shop-within-a-stores should be placed within those retail establishments that have developed a loyal following for a specific brand. Not limiting this type of marketing effort to the larger stores can significantly increase your sales.

☞ Give Them a Hand

Grand openings, expansions, moving sales…all of these attract a great deal of customer attention, and create a prime opportunity for you.

Any time that a store opens, expands, or has any type of special promotion, you have an opportunity to offer promotional items, merchandise, contest giveaways, imprinted bags, and refreshments.

Ideally, you'll start this relationship from the very first day by participating in the grand opening and keep it up throughout the years.

☞ Bring in the Reserves

During major events, grand openings, and other promotional events, retailers are hard pressed to find good sales floor staff. Their own staff might be very good, yet overwhelmed by the crowds at the special event.

Retailers really appreciate extra sets of hands to supplement their own staff. Any way you can assist helps cement the relationship.

☞ How Is Your Own Preferred Customer Program Working?

Preferred customer programs have become the number-one form of consumer direct mail advertising. This popularity is due to the increased sales that come from such pinpointed marketing. Loyal customers are presented with prime offers that the retailers know will appeal.

The concept works just as well between a vendor and a retailer. By knowing what your own customers' preferences are, right down to the time they like to be called or what they like to buy, you can tap into this information resource to pinpoint your marketing efforts.

☞ Observe Frequency Incentives

You already know how important it is to reward your best customers — but who are your best customers? They're not necessarily the ones who spend the most money, believe it or not.

Although the larger retailer may spend a lot of money placing one order a year, the smaller retailer who consistently places small orders and who reorders weekly or monthly is considered by many to be the better customer. Let these retailers know how important they are to you. Be sure to reward your customers based on their frequency of purchases.

Make sure your retailers understand this concept as well. While most small retailers understand the idea of "treat your better customers better," they don't necessarily know who their better customers are. Take a few minutes to explain the value of the frequent shopper and brainstorm ways that your retailer could reward those customers.

☞ Go to the Top

"You can't do business locked up in an ivory tower," says Steve Lang. "You have to be in touch with your customers. Get out there, talk to them, know what their problems are." Before Lang started Mon Cheri, he spent a year on the road, talking to small retailers and learning about the challenges they face. "That was one of the single smartest things I could have done," he explains. "It really gave me an understanding of who my customers are."

While not every company owner can spend a year on the road, all should have an easy, direct way to connect with their customers. Consider having an 800-number for retailers that plays a recorded message from the president of your company inviting the retailer to tell him or her the good, the bad, and the ugly, or to suggest how your company can improve.

As a nice touch, have the president return each call on a random basis. If there are too many calls, have a special assistant to the president contact the callers to thank them and ensure them that action will be taken on their comments.

☞ Retailing Scholarships

There are numerous retail education opportunities offered by specific trade associations, as well as the National Retail Federation. These opportunities offer real value to retailers, yet they are expensive.

Show a retailer you really care by offering a free scholarship to attend one of these educational forums. This can be an annual award program announced at a tradeshow as well as through your website, newsletters, and e-zines.

Accompany this gesture with an adequate public relations effort that co-brands the local retailer with you and is promoted through the retailer's local newspaper. Make an investment in education.

☞ Send Airline Tickets

Select a retailer who never attends tradeshows because of the cost, and offer a free airline ticket to attend a major tradeshow. This allows your customer to see the complete product line or lines, completely justifying the money you spent on the tickets.

The other twist to this concept is to have two or three vendors used by the same retailer share the expense of the ticket.

☞ Free Samples

Free is the best price. Free works. It's how you can entice retailers to try out your merchandise. It's difficult to say "no" when handed something for nothing, no strings attached.

"Offering a free sample can make all the difference," says Dana Lurie from Mon Cheri. "Especially in my industry, where retailers are accustomed to paying for sample dresses, to have someone offer that sample dress for free makes all the difference."

Occasionally, samples are used in lieu of other forms of payment. If a retailer chooses to participate in an ad campaign, for example, they may appreciate some free sample merchandise more than cooperative advertising funds.

Free samples can soften sales resistance. Sometimes all it takes to change a retailer's mind or attitude about a manufacturer and its merchandise is having the product in the store.

☞ It's More Than Just Cash

So far, the retailer incentives discussed here have been focused on cash savings or additional merchandise. However, many vendors have opted to give prize incentives instead.

One of the most popular is the ocean cruise, especially when the giveaway occurs on specific dates so all the winners travel together, along with your key personnel. One benefit of having the vendor aboard is it offers a prime opportunity to get to know the accounts better.

Moreover, if any business is conducted, such as a retail educational seminar, it can make the trip tax deductible. Otherwise, recipients are legally obligated to pay taxes on the free trip.

☞ Send a Needy Retailer to a Show

Reward your retailers for their purchases throughout the year by applying a percentage of their purchases toward the cost of their attending your annual tradeshow or conference.

Make sure to constantly yet subtly remind your retailers that you're doing this. One wholesaler gives retailers individual certificates indicating how much of their hotel bill and meals have been prepaid. Another vendor lists this information on each and every invoice.

Of course, retailers can redeem their certificates only by attending the tradeshow, where they are highly likely to write additional purchase orders.

☞ "Frequent Buyer Status" for Different Levels of Customers

Not all customers are created equal. Some customers are more valuable than others, yet many vendors in retail have not figured this out or acknowledged their better customers.

This isn't true in other industries, particularly the airline industry. By categorizing customers, they offer a platinum member more perks than a gold member. Thus, gold members work harder to earn the platinum level, know what they have to do to get there, and are motivated to stay with the same airline.

Consider recognizing your retailers with a similar system. Most retailers do not know how good an account they are for the vendor. They have no idea if their business really "matters."

☞ Clubs – A New Item a Month

Many kinds of monthly buying programs are offered by vendors. The obvious benefit to the vendor is that new orders are generated every month. The benefit to the retailer is that fresh items are coming in monthly.

These automatic programs work in various ways. Some vendors introduce new styles or models, such as in apparel, collectible, and gift lines in which manufacturers are constantly adding new items. Some automatically ship from a selection of off-price merchandise — guaranteeing the vendor a small monthly stream of orders.

Terms vary greatly. Some vendors allow unsold merchandise to be returned within a short period of time; some allow no returns of promotional or off-price merchandise. Whatever terms you offer, make sure that your retailers are made aware of and understand these terms at the time they enroll in the club.

☞ Contest for Best Displays

Sponsor an annual contest for the retailer who creates the best display of your merchandise. To increase the number of winners, increase the number of categories, such as: Best window display, best spot display, and best use of fixturing. Consider awarding a high-profile grand prize to the retailer who does the best job displaying your merchandise over the course of a year.

Contest criteria should be clearly posted, perhaps on your website. These criteria might spell out the use of props or signage supplied by you. Retailers can enter by e-mailing digital pictures to your company.

☞ Retailers and Vendors That Play Together, Stay Together

Here's a twist on the retailer retreat that is also a mini-tradeshow or educational event: the cruise that puts retailer winners together with the vendor's key personnel for some days of fun in the sun.

This travel incentive for retailers has no agenda other than having a good time and being together with retailers from other parts of the country that sell your merchandise. The friendships that form around these common ties can produce indirect benefits for the vendor.

☞ Create Your Own Credit Card

Plastic cards have slowly but surely invaded every corner of the business world. Most vendors now accept payments from their retailers with credit cards. This is a win/win situation, because the retailers can choose to stretch out the payments without hassle (beyond the monthly interest charges) and the vendor gets out of the credit business and enjoys a more regular cash flow.

Sometimes the manufacturer joins forces with a credit card vendor to create its own credit card. This increases the credit limit for the retailers, who are unlikely to put personal purchases on their business cards. The other benefit is having retailers walking around with your credit card in their wallets.

☞ Chase's Calendar of Events

Retailers are always looking for a good reason to have a sale or promotion. I listed the very best ones I could find in my book *The 5,000 Best Sale & Promotional Names & Ideas Ever Compiled* — and that's just scratching the surface.

Any vendor can develop their own, unique special occasion for its retailers and have it recognized as an international event by *Chase's Calendar of Events*, the go-to source for those searching for unique holidays and celebrations.

Chase's also serves as an unlimited source of existing promotional themes and events to piggyback. The best part is that there is no cost to you for having your event recognized.

Additionally, I've created a free downloadable e-book of *The 5,000 Best Sale & Promotional Names & Ideas Ever Compiled* you can use for this purpose. You can find it at www.ricksegel.com.

☞ Make Your Catalog a Selling Tool

"People pay attention to images," says Sal Macaluso. "They know the difference between an amateur effort and when things are professionally done. There's a reason that graphic artists make $500 an hour and models make $1,000 an hour."

Use the best resources you can to put together a dynamic, engaging catalog. When you prepare your catalog to show retailers, take the time to design one for your retailers to share with their customers.

Make sure the photos are taken to appeal to consumers and the copy is written to resemble a print advertisement. Copy is king — what you say in those little blurbs under the image has the power to generate tremendous sales. Omit prices in the consumer version, of course!

The Five Key Points You Need to Know

Point Number One: Promotion Doesn't Mean Sale!

Help your retailers design non-sale events that will generate sales without having to drop prices! Educational seminars, fun contests, celebrity events — all of these can be used to bring the crowds in and the profits up.

Point Number Two: The Power of the Press

Editorial coverage is ten times more valuable than advertising. Help your retailers show up in the local paper by teaching them how to use press releases effectively. You can even supply press releases your retailers can use!

Point Number Three: Visual Merchandising Is Critical

Displaying merchandise effectively is the hardest challenge for many retailers. Anything you can do to help them overcome this will be valued: in-store assistance, tip sheets or guides for great displays, even educational seminars teaching merchandising strategies specific to your products.

Point Number Four: Treat Your Better Customers Better

The retailer who consistently orders from you is a treasure. Make sure you're going out of your way to make life particularly pleasant for those retailers by offering special incentives, free shipping, etc.

Point Number Five: Support Retailers as They Improve

Provide scholarships to tradeshows or educational seminars, help fund airline tickets or transportation costs whatever it takes to demonstrate that you are the vendor who wants the retailer to truly succeed!

How can I apply what I've learned?

CHAPTER SIX

On the Web

There are more low-cost or no-cost
marketing tools available today
than even existed three years ago.
— Rick Segel —

☞ What the Retailer Knows

The Internet has transformed the way we do business. Consumers are increasingly comfortable shopping online and the Internet is the number-one place the public goes to research a major purchase.

Most retailers know that they need an Internet presence, but large numbers of retailers aren't sure exactly what that means or how they can make the most of their time online. Faced with having to spend hundreds of dollars for a website they don't "get," many retailers opt out of the Internet, which can have catastrophic consequences for their business — and eventually yours.

There are two ways that vendors can use the web to their benefit: making their website a valuable tool for their retailers and assisting their retailers in creating and maintaining a web presence that appeals to their target audience. In this chapter, we'll cover both of these topics.

☞ Begin at the Beginning

Depending on your industry, you may run into retailers who use little or no technology in the operation of their business. They may not have a computer — there are some who don't even have a fax machine.

Persuading these retailers that embracing technology will make their lives easier may be the toughest sales job of your entire life. Some retailers are leery of technology they don't understand, while others are loathe to spend the money on a computer when they perceive no clear benefit.

However, it's a fact of life that to enhance profitability and make business easier, computers are a necessity. Gently and consistently press that point. Show, rather than tell, by using your own computer whenever possible. Eventually you'll win the day.

(That's when you can start the next step: convincing them they need an e-commerce site!)

☞ Understand Your Website's Purpose

Every vendor should have a website, and every website should have a purpose. When the web was in its infancy, simply having a website was an accomplishment. Now vendors not only need to have a website, they need to know what they want that website to do and how they're going to accomplish it.

There are two types of websites for vendors. There's the B to B level, the business to business website. This is simply a website that vendors maintain for the use and reference of their retailers. This is a great place to store information, product specs, company updates, advertising resources, and more.

Then there's the B to C level. This is a business to consumer website. As I've stated before, the majority of manufacturers have no interest or inclination to do business directly with consumers. However, by providing a business to consumer website, the vendor can provide a valuable resource—for its customers, and more importantly, for its retailers.

It's important to realize that almost every major purchase Americans make today begins with a research segment that takes place online. For example, over 90 percent of the women getting married this year began searching for their dream gown online. The same holds true for customers in search of a car, golf clubs, lawn equipment, and more.

A manufacturer's website is an ideal way to showcase a product line. It builds brand awareness and allows consumers to make up their mind about what they want long before they set a single foot in the store. A good website can pre-sell the retailer's customers for them.

Providing links to retailers who carry your products, searchable by zip code, makes it easy for consumers to find the brick and mortar store most convenient for them. Additionally, if you can connect to your retailers' online sites, the customer can experience the ultimate in convenience — you sell another unit, and the retailer enjoys an effortless sale. Everybody wins.

☞ Help Your Retailers Get Online

The value of your website is enhanced when you can link to great websites belonging to your retailers. This can be challenging if your retailers don't have great websites — or websites at all!

At a minimum, you can help your retailers establish a web presence by connecting them with the people who are qualified and competent to do so. Create a list of recommended web designers and hosts that understand the challenges of small, independent retailers who are perhaps not the most tech-savvy.

Don't be shy about recommending this list to retailers who already have websites. It can be a great tool to help them make the most out of their sites.

Vet the professionals on this list carefully and update it often.

☞ Avoid the "Black Hole"

"Simply being online is not enough," says Linda Rigano of ThomasNet, which specializes in working with vendors who market to industrial buyers. "There's no sense driving traffic to your site if you're driving people into a black hole. Our customers' buyers have very specific needs. If they're looking at a product, they want detailed information, including product specifications.

"For a long time, suppliers didn't understand what their customers wanted," she adds. "This has been, for us, a trend led by the engineers."

Ask yourself what type of detailed information your customers want to know. What questions do your customers have? More importantly, can they find the answers on your website?

"Buying online is a buyer-led process," Rigano says. "Your customers are telling you, by their searches, what they want. This is very different from the traditional model. The market has changed."

In the same vein, you want to make sure that your retailers are registered with Google local and other location-driven search engines.

☞ Realize the Value of Your Website as a Branding Tool

"A website is one of the most powerful branding tools a small company can have," says Paul Garbino, also of ThomasNet. "The user experience is the most important part of that branding experience."

What goes into a user experience? A number of things. "The better the site organization, the better the navigation, the better the site looks, the better the user's experience is going to be," Garbino says. Website visitors assess these criteria, sometimes unconsciously. This assessment plays a pivotal role in how the company views you. The better job you do presenting yourself online, the more favorably the retailer will view your organization.

☞ Make Your Website Easy to Use

"I've seen a lot of websites," says Stephen Situm of Stephen Vincent Wines. "They're quite beautiful. I'm sure they cost lots of money. But they're difficult to use." That difficulty is a problem for Stephen and other retailers. "My time is money too. I don't have a half-hour to spend trying to figure out some other guy's website."

It's always a good idea to "test drive" your website by having people wholly unfamiliar with your company and products attempt to navigate it before taking it live. Another factor that makes your website easy to use is incorporating accepted website layout features: navigation bars along the left or bottom of the screen, easily found site maps, and contact information on every page.

☞ Act Globally, Think Locally

A website can reach customers all over the world. However, it's important to remember that those customers have some very local concerns.

When you're connecting a customer with the retailer closest to her, make sure to provide her with as much information as humanly possible. This includes the store's location and phone number, as well as its website and e-mail. If possible, include a map to the store, or at a minimum, link to an online direction site.

Remember, customers can't shop in brick and mortar stores if they can't find brick and mortar stores. Additionally, they won't look for directions. You've got to make it as easy and effortless as possible for them to find your retailers.

☞ Understand How Your Customers Find You

There are a number of ways that retailers find websites. "One way is through traditional advertising," says Rigano. "Use print, web, and other advertising to direct people to your website." Another route is via search engines, such as Google. Making the most of search engine results can be accomplished via search engine optimization techniques and pay per click advertising.

If you cater to a specific niche market, Rigano suggests, you'll also want to make sure that your company's website is easily found through a "destination site" search function. "If one of our clients' customers is looking for titanium," she explains, "he's not going to go to Google. Google won't help him. That'll turn up science sites talking about the periodic table, and jewelry sites featuring titanium rings—it'll take him forever to sort through all that." By going to a destination site, retailers know that their search results will be relevant to them, which is a great timesaver that busy business owners appreciate.

☞ Copy Is King, and the Headline Is the Emperor

The number-one principle of search engine optimization is "Copy Is King." Even more important are headlines, both those that head an article and internal headlines within the copy. Simply listing relevant keywords on your site in the hopes that search engines will find you is an exercise in futility.

Posting content with real value—informative or entertaining content, product descriptions, and information that retailers will want to know — offers you the best of both worlds: a site that will be "read" by search engines and be pleasing to retailers who are directed there.

Use many headlines! Book designers know this: When they want an easy-to-read book, they break the copy up in small paragraphs and use lots of headlines. This is the primary model for web text — use it on your site!

"Remember," Rigano says, "SEO is not for free. It's simply the icing on the cake. The content has always been the cake itself and it always will be."

☞ Have Your Contact Information On Every Page

Every single page of your website should have a "Contact Us" button or link. Never assume that retailers will come to your homepage first. Specific search engine results or clicking through links may bring retailers to pages within your site — often directly to certain merchandise that they'd been searching for.

Make it easy for retailers to buy what they've been looking for, or at least find more information. Have a "Contact Us" button or link on every page. This can offer an e-mail address or an entire contact page with mailing address, phone and fax numbers, and e-mail information. The more information you offer, the better off you are. There are still retailers out there who don't mind searching for information over the web, but want to do their buying in person.

Remember, web users grow more impatient with every generation. Retailers will expect a certain minimum level of sophistication from your site. If they find that it's not easy to navigate, lacks certain essential information, or is just too slow, you won't get the benefit of the doubt. They're already moving on, to another company with a site that can keep up with them.

☞ Eliminate Registration Requirements

While your retailers want to be able to find you easily, they don't necessarily want you to find them. Retailers want to remain anonymous, according to Rigano, and a registration requirement scares them off.

"Stop asking for information," she says. "I can't tell you how many times we've had clients take the registration requirement off, and their traffic increases." People don't mind giving their information if they see the value of doing so, but divulging their identity, e-mail, and other information for no clear reward is a definite turn-off.

☞ Cater to the Competitive

Many people like to participate in competitive games and quizzes, and everyone likes to have fun. Consider devoting some space on your website for a multiple choice quiz or trivia contest that's open only to your retailers.

For the best of both worlds, you can make this quiz educational in nature. Post winners' names or have a points system to encourage friendly competition among your retailers. Consider awarding monthly prizes to keep people engaged, and change the content often to keep them interested!

☞ Be Careful of Links

Connecting your customers with the appropriate retailers is qualitatively different from linking to your retailers' websites. You never, ever, ever want to link directly from your website to theirs.

Why?

It's far too easy for links to go bad. You have no idea where a link is going. What may appear to go to an innocuous gift shop, for example, can easily be redirected to a website with objectionable content. You never, ever want to create even the flimsiest connection between your manufacturer's website and anything of that nature.

Additionally, even if the link goes to the retailer as intended, who knows what your customer will find there? You may be bringing your customers to a generic retailer's homepage, where they're advertising your products — and that of your competitor!

It is a huge burden to monitor links. Relieve yourself of this burden by providing contact information to your retailers without allowing direct links.

☞ Create a Download Center

In the retailers-only section of your website, or on the B2B version of your website, create a download center. Retailers can visit this area to download pictures, logos, text, and more to create their own high-quality, customized ads, fliers, and brochures. They choose what merchandise they want to feature and the related text and pictures they favor. Then it's simply a matter of cutting and pasting the elements into a layout.

Want to go the extra mile? Store the retailer's own logos on your site to complete the ad and make it truly effortless for your retailers.

The download center is also a great place to store educational materials. If you have a special report, best practices white paper, or other informational material you'd like your retailers to read, make it available as a downloadable PDF. E-mail alerts can let your retailers site before the conversion action, they're gone forever. Know when something new and exciting has been put on the site.

☞ Measure Your Results

"You can't manage what you can't measure," says know how much business you're losing." Rigano. "If you can't track results from your website, you might as well not have one."

Critical to measuring your results, of course, is having a clear understanding of what you want those end results to be. "Take a step back," Rigano says. "Ask yourself: *Who am I trying to reach with this website? What do I want to do? What do I want to know about the people visiting my site?*"

Often, the desired result is what web experts call a conversion action: a step that brings the retailer, in this case, closer to the vendor. It may be calling for more information, or e-mailing a sales representative, or even placing an order online. No matter what your desired conversion action is, you need to have a clear strategy to get website visitors to that point, and measure how many visitors go through the conversion process and how many leave your site without doing so.

"Remember, your biggest competitor is the back button!" says Rigano. Often, if a customer leaves your site before the conversion action, they're gone forever. Additionally, 65 percent of people who have a negative experience on a website never return to that site. But if you don't know they're leaving, you can't repair the problems that drive this traffic away. That's why measurement is critical. "Otherwise," Rigano concludes, "you'll never know how much business you are losing."

The Five Key Points You Need to Know

Point Number One: Make It Easy The best websites are easy to find, easy to navigate, easy to understand. Review your website often. Can someone who has never been there before find what they need quickly and easily?

Point Number Two: Support Your Retailers' Online Efforts Help your retailers have an online presence. Connect them with the professionals they need to get started.

Point Number Three: Copy Is King! Pay careful attention to the language you use on your website and company blog as that's how search engines find you! Strategic use of headlines makes this work even better!

Point Number Four: Put Your Contact Information on Every Page You never know how customers are going to find you. Make sure your contact information is on every single web page.

Point Number Five: Make Your Website a Resource Your website can be a great resource. Offer downloadable signs, advertising ideas, management resources, merchandise information, and more. Make this accessible only to your registered retailers — this isn't for the general consumer.

How can I apply what I've learned?

CHAPTER SEVEN

Tradeshows
Planning, Promotion and People

If you want word of mouth advertising
then give people something to talk about.
— Rick Segel —

☞ What the Retailer Knows

Tradeshows are major events. Many retailers do more buying during these two- to three-day events than they do at any other time of the year. Making face to face contact with the people behind the merchandise is important to many retailers, as is getting good information about what's new, what's hot, and what will work well in their stores.

Every second counts at a tradeshow. It's a crowded, over-whelming environment, but there are steps you can take to stand out from the masses and make yourself more appealing to retailers. This section is divided into five sections: Planning, Promotion, People, At the Show, and After the Show. Each component is critical.

Together they form a powerhouse strategy guaranteed to make you the vendor of choice.

PLANNING

☞ Location, Location, Location

Location is paramount for brick and mortar stores, and it's no less important when you're competing for show floor real estate. Never stop asking the show organizers what the requirements are to secure the best floor space. It may require having an exhibit of a certain size or making certain sponsorship commitments.

Favored exhibiting spots almost always include the end of aisles, the first booth people see when entering an exhibition area, and booths near food service areas.

Booths near restrooms are a mixed blessing: You may get a lot of traffic in that area, but much of those people have other things besides shopping on their minds.

☞ Move into the Right Neighborhood

When you're selecting exhibit space, ask show organizers to situate you near complementary vendors. Being close to your competitors is far, far better than being placed in an aisle with merchandise nothing like yours.

Securing positioning like this is seldom easy to accomplish. You may not be able to pull it off if you're new to a show or if you wait until the last minute to reserve your space. However, you should never stop trying. Being a squeaky wheel has its advantages, especially if you want to get noticed at a show!

👉 Consider All the Senses

When you're selecting display space, consider all the senses. Shoppers make selections largely with their eyes, but don't forget the other four senses.

Vision: Will attendees be able to see your booth, or will you be obscured by a support pillar? Will you be visually overwhelmed by the display next to yours, a spectacular view, or an entrance/exit doorway? Is your booth cluttered with merchandise?

Hearing: Don't forget sounds. The noise from heating and cooling systems, delivery areas, and busy hallways can make a display unattractive. Background music is always nice, as long as it is not too loud to affect the neighboring exhibits. Use it to set a mood.

Smell: Bad smells don't sell! Strong scents, such as those that may come from a food service or restroom area, can turn off buyers. It's hard to make good purchasing decisions if a bad smell is turning your stomach. This is especially true for those of you in the food or beverage industry, where taste is paramount.

There are multiple products on the market you can use to put good scents into the air at your display, but proceed with caution. What one person loves in a smell can repel another. Increasing numbers of people are allergic to perfume and scented room deodorizers. The safest scent is something fresh and clean.

Taste: Appealing to the attendees' taste buds can be as simple as offering hard candies or M&M's or as elaborate as specially-baked cookies. Offer refreshments that are in alignment with the quality of the merchandise you're selling. If you are selling high-quality merchandise, reflect that quality in your giveaways. If there's a clever way to use the refreshments to reinforce your company's image, with a logo design or so on, so much the better.

Touch: Attendees often like to touch the merchandise. Is your exhibit space large enough that they'll be able to indulge their tactile desires? Crowding too much merchandise into too small of a space makes this impossible and deprives attendees of a critical purchasing resource.

Explore Mentorship Programs

Show organizers want their exhibitors to succeed. One way they do this is by facilitating mentorship programs — partnering veteran exhibitors who have lots of tradeshow experience with those new to the show floor. This is a prime opportunity to get "insider information" from someone who is really in the know.

Seeking out exhibiting mentorship programs has an additional benefit. You'll be able to network with peers and colleagues, gaining a greater understanding and appreciation of who else is in the marketplace. This can ultimately be of great use to your customers. They might have a need that your company can't fulfill, but you'll know exactly where to send them!

"Our experienced exhibitors love the mentorship program as much as the new exhibitors," says Tony Orlando, George Little Management. "You never know when you're going to learn something valuable. Both parties benefit from the relationship tremendously."

Seek out show management and ask them about mentoring opportunities. Whether you're a pro on the show floor or still learning the ropes, you'll be glad that you did!

☞ Design Your Exhibit Floor Plan Carefully

Buyers make decisions with their eyes. If two displays are selling identical merchandise, the majority of attendees will go to the display that has the product attractively displayed in an inviting atmosphere.

Plan your traffic flow carefully. Where will your displays be set up? Where will your tables go? Can people move around the display easily without feeling trapped or claustrophobic? How easily can people enter and exit? Can your staffers see every corner of the exhibit?

Make it easy for someone to come into your booth, feel comfortable enough to stay there, and write an order without feeling like the entire world is looking over their shoulder. Make sure it's easy to leave your booth—people don't like feeling trapped.

Never, ever settle for putting merchandise in the back with a table and two chairs in the front of the display. That's not welcoming. In fact, it creates a barrier between you and your attendees—exactly the opposite of the welcoming impression you want to create.

☞ Open Wide

Your exhibit should be arranged like a funnel, with the widest, largest opening to the aisle or entrance to the booth. Large, open spaces are inviting and make visitors feel like there's plenty of room for them to enter comfortably.

If people feel like they're going to be crowded or smooshed against colleagues, they'll opt not to enter the space. No one likes to be jostled about. Ensure enough space for your guests to move freely.

The purpose of a wide entrance is to create an inviting feeling while being less intimidating, just as a grocery store has a lobby area as you enter.

☞ Think Vertically

Consider expanding the height of your display above the traditional 8-foot height of the pipe and drape. This could have several advantages, especially if your exhibit is "buried" in the middle of an aisle. Attendees view the show floor from a distance, so anything elevated immediately stands out and attracts attention.

Make sure to ask show organizers before "going up." Some shows do not allow this kind of one-up-manship, but there are just as many shows that have no policy on it at all.

What do you put up high? Consider banners, streamers, or colorful flags. Bright colors attract attention and can be a powerful branding tool. If you can, elevated signage is always a plus. You're letting crowds know who and where you are—and conveying a constant if subtle marketing message the whole time.

☞ Look Down

"Floor coverings are one of those subtle things that make an exhibit stand out," says Orlando. "You might not think that anyone would notice the carpeting, but they really do."

Talk to show organizers and find out what your options are. This may include using a different color carpet from other exhibitors, or using custom cuts of carpet to create a logo design.

Think comfort. Attendees have been walking on hard concrete floors for hours. What will they think once they step onto your cushiony soft carpet? Be careful with laminate or faux-wood flooring. These surfaces look nice but can be treacherously slippery in high-traffic areas. Additionally, they're difficult to keep looking clean.

☞ Display Merchandise as in the Store

Never forget who tradeshow attendees are: retailers who have to sell your products to the customer. Too often, manufacturers create beautiful displays that have absolutely no connection with the way retailers actually merchandise the product in the store.

Create displays that are easily adaptable to a store setting. Retailers will want to copy the idea for their own shops. Make it easy for them by offering documentation or photographs so they can duplicate the displays themselves. Additionally, if your company offers any retailer support (displays, signage, etc.), don't miss this opportunity to mention it. It might be the one factor that brings a retailer's business your way.

☞ Use the Booth Display as a Store Prototype

Create your exhibit using the fixtures, signs, and display techniques that retailers can purchase through you. Give them more than a product — provide an entire selling package they can use to drive business. Remember, by giving retailers maximum profitability for minimal effort, you're positioning yourself as the preferred vendor.

Your goal is to create the optimum fixture/display presentation to maximize sell-through of your products. Offer solutions and ideas to the retailer. Make it easy. Provide copies of blueprints for store-building purposes. Let your retailers know where they can access these design and promotional materials online.

☞ Down in Front

Arrange the merchandise in your exhibit so it cascades from the rear. Do this by positioning the tallest merchandise in the back and the shortest in front. If all of your merchandise is of a similar size, use risers or other fixtures to elevate the product at the back of the booth.

Doing so allows visitors who are walking the aisles to see all of your offerings at a glance. This will enable them to decide quickly if you have something they're interested in. Time is of the essence at tradeshows. Give all of your products a chance by ensuring that they're visible. A retailer won't be interested in your merchandise if she can't see it!

☞ Fixture: Friend or Foe

Use caution when incorporating fixtures in your display space. Be careful not to block pathways with fixtures. Not only do such displays restrict passage, but the displays also run the risk of causing constant bumping and jarring.

However, interesting and striking fixtures can attract attention. If you can capture someone's interest, if even for a moment, it gives you a chance to engage her in conversation and start relationship building.

Careful placement is key. If you have a distinctive fixture and want to incorporate it into your booth, make sure it is ideally located. Keep traffic moving freely and don't stray outside of your designated display space.

☞ Remove Roadblocks

Avoid using a table at the front of the booth as your desk. Doing so looks unprofessional and demonstrates a fundamental lack of understanding about the exhibiting process. It doesn't look inviting at all. You're putting a bar across your front door!

Not only is this off-putting, it blocks the path to the merchandise. Exhibit goers seldom stop at booths that have intentional obstacles like this. If they do stop, they don't linger and interact with the merchandise.

Retailers need an opportunity to look at the merchandise before they make the commitment to sit down and write an order. Don't stand in their way!

☞ Think Like a Shopper

When you're setting up merchandise in an exhibit, consider how your attendees will view it. This is another time when you can mirror the way retailers might display the merchandise in your store.

With that in mind, you don't want to position merchandise too high, where people have to stretch to see it. On the other hand, you don't want to go too low. Display merchandise at least 30 inches off the floor. If you go lower than this, visitors will have to bend over to view the products. This is often uncomfortable, and on a pragmatic level, takes up additional space in your booth.

☞ Make the Rear of Your Exhibit a Magnet

Retailer designers work hard to get customers from the front of the store to the back wall. Take the best of what they know and apply it to your exhibit. Put an eye-catching attraction at a higher elevation near the rear of your booth.

This will draw the retailer into your exhibit. It is much easier to engage with and talk to retailers while they're in "your" space. Additionally, you'll have less interference from aisle traffic.

Play to the attendees' curiosity. Use something vivid and engaging, such as a new product, a logo, or creative signage.

☞ It's More Than Window Dressing

Image is everything when it comes to tradeshows. Decisions to visit a booth or pass it by are made in the blink of an eye. If your booth isn't eye-catching, attractive, and inviting, your customers will opt to go somewhere else.

That's why it's well worth it to hire a professional to decorate your booth. It makes a difference. The pros have the skills and know-how to create a distinctive environment. Customers want different and exciting, so give them that.

Remember, tradeshows are more than simple selling. It's show biz. It's a little bit theatrical, a little bit three ring circus. Standing out in that environment is difficult. Professional decorating can give you that added edge that you need.

☞ Consistency Is Key

When you're designing your booth, remember, whatever your product, make sure its setting is in alignment with your retailers' vision, image, and expectations. They know what their customers are looking for. You have this chance to prove that you're it.

For example, let's say you're selling skateboards. You wouldn't want a pastoral, calm display. That's not what your target audience is about. Instead, your booth has to look young, hip, bright, and extreme. You want the music loud and the personnel urban chic.

Your setting must match expectations. Incorporate all of your skills and know-how into delivering the booth your retailers expect — plus a little bit more!

☞ Use Booth Identification Signage

Think of your exhibit as your storefront. You'd never consider having a store with no exterior signage, would you? Yet many exhibitors do exactly that.

You need booth identification signage. These signs need to be visible from every possible angle, so retailers on the floor can quickly and easily identify you. The majority of tradeshow exhibitors fail to do this, opting instead to rely upon the identification signage provided by the exhibit hall. Don't be lazy!

Consider floor signage. Angled signs that stand 2 feet to 4 feet in height take advantage of the fact that people walking by a booth are not generally looking up. Use bright colors and strong graphics to attract attention. If you lack signage at this point, you're missing a prime opportunity to lure in retailers.

Bring all your own identifying signs and make sure to include them within your display.

☞ Signage Is Good Service

Do you want to connect more concretely and effectively with retailers at the tradeshow? USE SIGNAGE! Signage is the single most powerful way you can enhance your exhibit.

Signage within your exhibit can act as a silent sales force. Use signs to identify your company, your products, and most importantly, critical information about your merchandise. Signage can provide the reason to buy! Your signs can communicate with your retailers for you!

Ask yourself What are the most common questions retailers come to us with? Spell out the answers on your signs! This demonstrates to the retailer that you care about and understand some of their concerns and are willing to go the extra mile to make their lives easier.

Retailers who shop tradeshows regard signage as a form of good service—the same way the consumer regards the signage in a store.

☞ Display Your Ads

Creative, provocative, image-building, and even controversial advertisements make great posters. Great posters make great tradeshow displays.

Using ads as posters reinforces the ad, creates consistency, aligns your booth with the product, and shows your merchandise the way it is intended to be shown. Additionally, it makes it easy for retailers to envision how the public sees your product and how they could position your merchandise within their stores.

Don't be afraid to offer your retailers copies of the poster—or better yet, have them delivered directly to the retailers' stores! You'd be amazed how many retailers will jump on this offer. Ads can be powerful selling tools, especially iconic ads like Guess Jeans, Calvin Klein underwear, or the long string of Absolut Vodka ads.

As an added bonus, posters are a relatively simple display prop. They're light and easy to ship and require no particular skill to put up, which is great for novice exhibitors.

☞ Embrace Signage Technology

High-tech solutions exist for almost everything today, and the electronic message board has certainly come of age. It is easier to program and change messages than with a printed sign. The key to an effective electronic message board is to not only inform but also cause the visitor to interact with the booth. On the sign, say who you are and what you sell.

Think fun! Boring signs do not sell! So have the signs ask a question. For example:

- Do you need X?

- Would you like X?

- When was the last time you X?

- Did you pay too much?

- Have you shopped everybody?

The goal is to create a moment of interaction. Facts tell, but stories sell!

☞ The Show Must Go on – Continuous DVD

Running a video at your booth isn't a new idea, but what you choose to run can differentiate you from other exhibitors. Most vendors run video of their product line, which is okay—but it's not thinking like a retailer.

Go the extra mile and show retailers how the product can be displayed or merchandised. This makes it more "real" for your customers and is far more practical and helpful. Show the retailer sample ads or the way the vendor recommends that the product be promoted. Again, this may help retailers envision how the merchandise will work in their stores.

Creative video that focuses on the retailer's perspective can be the deciding factor in whether or not the retailer decides to place an order for that merchandise.

☞ Keep It Moving!

If your exhibit contains products, displays, or props that move or must be turned on, make sure they work! This should be done before you leave for the show and at least daily upon arrival.

This is especially pertinent for display models. If a retailer wants to try out an item and it doesn't work, what do you think the chances are that the retailer will place an order? Not very good!

In an added note, keep extra batteries on hand for battery-driven merchandise. These items get a lot of use during a tradeshow and batteries die quickly. Use slow times to check display models and replace batteries as needed.

☞ Never Underestimate the Power of Lighting

The more light you can add to your exhibit, the more retailers you will attract. Lighting sells. This is a foolproof fact, no matter what setting you're in.

There is no excuse for not having the proper spotlights and lighting treatments. The size of the equipment is so small and the costs so reasonable that even the smallest of exhibitors can properly light their offerings.

Lighting can also be used to create special features, such as image projectors that display your logo or message on the ceilings, walls, or floors of the exhibit hall.

Make sure to check with show management to see if there are any lighting restrictions for a given exhibit space.

☞ Create a Theme Just for Your Booth

Tradeshows have themes, so why can't you? During the planning stages, select a theme for your booth. Design your display to incorporate this theme, from décor to costumes to giveaway items.

Promote this theme heavily during your pre-show marketing. You can even make the theme part of an incentive campaign, encouraging guests to stop by your Hawaiian Luau, for example, or to look for the North Pole.

Selecting and promoting a theme, especially when your booth team is excited and engaged about the idea, can generate tremendous buzz on the show floor. One attendee will tell another about what you're doing and before you know it, you've got all kinds of word-of-mouth advertising.

☞ Tie into the Tradeshow Theme

If you're exhibiting at a show that has a theme, use that theme in your booth in as many ways as possible. Incorporate the theme into your display, your signage, your decorations, even your snacks! Use the theme when selecting your booth staff's attire.

Even if this tactic doesn't impress your buyers, it will certainly impress the show organizers who came up with the theme. This is a good thing, considering they're the ones who will be referring attendees to take a look at your booth. Additionally, when the time comes to decide next year's booth placement, they're going to remember your efforts and may very well reward you with a better location.

One vendor we've seen has built a reputation by consistently tying into the theme of the tradeshow, making his booth a "must-see" for every buyer. The interpretation of the show theme and its implementation makes this booth a true show-stopper.

PROMOTION

☞ Wear the Pre-show Pin

Have a lapel pin or button designed that is colorful, easily distinguished, and bears a logo or phrase relating to your company. Have your sales team wear the button for the week prior to the show when making their sales calls. Give them buttons to distribute to their accounts.

Additionally, send the buttons in your pre-show mailers.

Invite your retailers to wear the pin during the show. When they come to your exhibit wearing the button, give them a nice gift. Make sure the gift is something that makes it worth the retailer's time to both remember and wear the button — it's the least that you can do, considering the amount of free advertising attendees are doing on your behalf while wearing the button!

Distinctive, eye-catching buttons can also serve to generate positive word-of-mouth publicity surrounding your exhibit. In the best-case scenario, attendees you haven't talked to before will want a button for themselves, and will come to the booth seeking one. You may attract customers you otherwise never would have gotten.

☞ Pre-show Mailings

Pre-show promotion is critical to your success. Send a mailing to your retailers clearly explaining why they should come to your booth. Remember: Most shows have hundreds of booths, and attendees have only a limited amount of time. Spell out why your booth is a must-see destination.

Clearly spell out what your show specials are. Incentives are a common part of the tradeshow environment, and most attendees expect to save money by shopping at the show. Let them know what they can expect from you and make sure these are real specials, not "make believe" bargains that will be available after the show. Nobody likes to be fooled that way!

Use mailings to announce new product launches that will be made at the show. This is a prime opportunity to spell out what the new product is, why the retailer might be interested in it, and what customer profile the product was designed for.

☞ Pre-show Calls

Take a moment to call your best customers — and those customers you wish were your best customers — before the show. This can be the make or break point for some attendees. Without that last minute reminder to visit a certain vendor, it's very likely that they'll simply forget to stop by that vendor's booth.

I call this the "out of sight, out of mind" syndrome. Tradeshows are overwhelming. There are hundreds of displays, filled with people who all want to talk to the attendee. If you're not front and center in that attendee's mind, it's more than likely that he'll be distracted by all the shiny demands on his attention.

Use your pre-show call to reinforce the show specials described in your mailing. This is also a prime time to make appointments for showing product lines and writing orders. Remember, put the focus on the buyer: What appointment times will work best for him? Simple courtesy can help you realize a real return on your tradeshow experience.

☞ Participate in Management's Promotional Efforts

Show organizers often set up promotional efforts at low or no cost to show participants. These efforts can range from special directory listings to artists' alleys and product walks and show preview space. Inquire ahead of time what special opportunities exist and how you can participate in them.

Show attendees often seek out the organizer's events as "the best of" or quick ways to get an overview of the show as a whole. Participating in these forums will get you in front of eyes that might otherwise never see you.

At the same time, being listed in special interest directories, such as those listing free trade vendors, makes you more attractive to those retailers who make decisions based upon those criteria.

☞ Schedule Book Signings at Your Booth

Find out who is speaking at your tradeshow and invite her to do a 30-minute book signing at your booth. She'll likely jump at the opportunity, and this is a great way to generate traffic. Many times, you'll be able to get the speaker to stay at your booth for a little while to meet your customers.

If you can invite a different speaker every day, your booth will quickly develop a reputation as the place where things are happening. Make sure to mention the signings in your pre-show promotional materials, on your website, and in communications with your retailers.

☞ Host Mini-Seminars at Your Booth

Invite experts who are well-known in your field to come to your booth and do presentations that will be of interest to retailers. These presentations can range from product presentations to display techniques to advertising and marketing strategies.

Set up chairs in your booth to limit attendance — not only because you don't have much room, but also because it will make retailers want to come back for the next event. When all the chairs are full, it generates excitement. People want to know what "everyone" is listening to.

As a nice touch, send special invitations to your retailers, letting them know about the seminars and encouraging them to attend. Personalize these, if at all possible, and let them know you'd love to see them at the seminar.

☞ The Guest Appearance

Arrange for one of your product designers to be at your booth to visit with retailers. The key is to announce the times that he or she will be available, promoting the event through postcards, press releases, your newsletter, and the show's daily bulletin board. You'd be surprised how many retailers are eager to meet the people behind the products.

You might even set up a digital camera and printer so retailers can have their pictures taken with the designer and get them autographed.

☞ Sponsor a Tradeshow Speaker

Tradeshows are starting to defray their own costs for professional speakers by having vendors sponsor them. There are many good reasons to consider this:

- Your company name is listed in every place the speaker's name is listed, including all pre-show mailings, all signage, and all tradeshow publications.

- You have the opportunity to hand out brochures about your product together with the speaker's handouts and to say a few words before the speaker starts.

- The speaker always thanks and recognizes the vendor's commitment to the education of their industry.

- The public relations benefit and positioning of your company are almost priceless, especially if sponsorship is done on a consistent basis.

Once you start to sponsor such an event, other vendors will jump on the bandwagon, so be the first—and anticipate a long-term commitment.

For more information on this, and many other topics, make sure to check out Susan Friedmann, The Tradeshow Coach. (www.thetradeshowcoach.com)

☞ Tradeshow Massage Therapy

Many tradeshows have a massage therapist for hire in the common areas of the exhibit hall. After walking through the crowds all day, many attendees really welcome the relief and restorative break a skilled massage therapist offers.

A welcome variation on this theme is to have a massage therapist at your booth for a couple of hours late in the day. These can be neck and shoulder massages, which require no more room than the chair the visitor sits in.

Buyers will come for the massage and stay longer than they ever intended. Make sure to promote the massage therapist's presence for maximum effect. You could even offer a "free massage with each order written."

☞ Giveaways

The best giveaways are attractive and visible. Give retailers something that they can put on their clothing during the show. Make sure the product is unique.

At a college book show, there was a vendor giving out felt stickers of favorite college teams. That was a vendor who understood the retailers he was dealing with! Avoid t-shirts or other promotional items that people cannot see during the show. The idea is to generate interest and buzz so other attendees can't help but come by your booth to get their own giveaway item!

The best giveaways are educational: those items that teach your retailers how to do something better. Visual merchandising tips are always welcome, as are tips on promoting and cost-affordable advertising. Focus on ways to help your retailers sell more.

☞ It's in the Bag

The shopping bag as a giveaway is an old trick, but it works best with this new twist. Instead of having only the vendor's name on the bag, add an introductory line such as: "I just saw the new line at Booth #X!" Put some sell into your bag.

The only word of caution I'm going to offer here is that if you are going to be preprinting bags with the booth number on it, make sure you have the correct number and that you don't order too many. You can't carry these bags over to another show.

Canvas bags are great but expensive. A good high-quality plastic or paper shopping bag can be just as effective. Make it BIG, so it's the biggest and heaviest bag that all the other bags are put into!

PEOPLE

🖝 People Buy People

"People buy people," says Stacey Heiss, Western Exhibitors. "Your staffers need to be interactive. You want a team that is standing up, upbeat, friendly, right out there. They need to have product knowledge to the nth degree: not only what your products are, but where they're made, what it takes to get them shipped, what the service situation is—the whole story."

Heiss reports seeing a profound difference in the type of questions buyers are asking, spurred by the changing questions retailers face from their customers. "That might be different, but one thing remains the same: It's your people who make the difference. Send the right people to the show."

🖝 Train Your Team

The skills needed to excel in the tradeshow environment are similar to but not exactly the same as the skills needed to do a superlative job as a salesperson in the field. Several factors are qualitatively different: You see more people, in less time, in a far more competitive environment at a tradeshow then you ever do in your day-to-day routine.

For this reason, training is essential. You want your sales team to deliver maximum results, so take the time to give them the skills they need to succeed. There are companies that specialize in providing this kind of training, such as The Tradeshow Coach.

Tradeshow training can ensure that your team is prepared with sales techniques that work best in situations where you have a very limited amount of time and an excess of competition. Additionally, the tradeshow environment comes with its own etiquette, from how to handle competitors who are prying for insider information to how to move along the "tire kickers" and goodie-hunters who attend every single show. Use training to learn how to generate positive word-of-mouth buzz surrounding your company. It's the best advertising money can't buy.

☞ Practice Makes Perfect

If your booth staffers are uncomfortable and ill at ease in the show booth, they'll communicate that discomfort to the public. It's extremely annoying for a buyer to shop a booth where the staffers obviously don't know the set-up. Attendees have very limited time at the show. They don't want to waste it watching your team look for product.

Eliminate both the discomfort and annoyance factors by having your team practice before the show. Set up a mock booth and role play live scenarios. This will both familiarize your team with merchandise placement and help them get comfortable in the booth.

If you have a sales team working at different tradeshows, standardize your booth. Use schematics to communicate set-up information, and give your team adequate time to learn the layout.

☞ Create a Dress Code

A vendor must look professional. Clothes can be a turn-off or a turn-on. Retailers will be drawn to those vendors who have a look that mirrors the image they themselves are trying to project.

Clothes that are too sexy, too sloppy, or too dirty will alienate the retailer and do incredible damage to your reputation. It is important to create a dress code for your staffers and clearly spell out what you expect them to wear on the show floor.

Increasingly, vendors are opting for logo-imprinted shirts or tops. This is a nice, safe solution, with one major drawback. All the vendors are starting to look alike with their embroidered denim shirts. Ideally, you want to do something different and distinct, while still projecting a professional image.

☞ Consider Costumes

Professional doesn't have to mean boring! If you really want to attract attention, add a creative flair to how your booth personnel dress. Costumes are great fun and they attract a great deal of attention on the show floor.

Depending on your product, a costume can be as simple as wearing white coats to look like doctors or a cap and gown to look like a professor. Obviously, you can go to much greater extremes, but even a tuxedo can go a long way toward setting a mood.

☞ Outsource Cautiously

Smaller vendors face a challenge when it comes to staffing tradeshows. Pulling their sales team out of the field for a week can be extremely difficult and can create a logistic nightmare. Yet the vendor doesn't want to miss out on the opportunity the tradeshow presents. Outsourcing the sales job is often the answer.

If you opt to outsource, spend the time and money to educate these people about your merchandise, your company, its policies, and its mission. Buyers have lots of questions, and they expect answers. Part of the reason retailers attend shows, after all, is to communicate directly with the folks who have extensive product knowledge. Give them more than a "pretty face" to talk to.

It'll never be possible to transform temporary help into industry experts. Teach your temporary team the proper way to respond to a question they don't know the answer to, which should include a follow-up protocol to ensure the questioner gets the information he wants in a timely fashion.

☞ Have Instant Answers

Maintain online access to your office so you can assist buyers with anything while they are at your booth. This includes accounting, shipping, and production.

This is especially critical if you're outsourcing some or all of your booth staffing positions. Make "When in doubt, check it out" your watchword. It's far better to have your reps e-mail you for a correct answer than to guess incorrectly!

☞ Create a Retail Advisory Panel

Don't be afraid to ask your retailers for their opinions. Their vast knowledge about the way to sell merchandise represents an untapped resource of expertise for you. As an added bonus, many retailers are flattered when asked to serve on such a panel.

Recruit six to ten panel members, each of whom demonstrates these qualifications:

- Is a tradeshow regular
- Runs a good business
- Is respected within the industry
- Is progressive
- Offers a different point of view

Plan a breakfast for your advisory panel members held once during the annual show for no more than 75 minutes. Pick their brains and get them to share ideas on topics ranging from their show experience to business trends to ways you can improve your business.

When ideas are shared in a group, people's combined energy inspires greater insight. You not only benefit from this powerhouse of ideas but also cement relationships.

☞ Every Opinion Counts

Less formal than the advisory group is to simply ask the retailers who visit your booth what they think of the booth and how you could improve it. Everyone loves a person who is humble enough to ask other people's opinions.

Survey the retailers who stop by your booth about specific topics. Polling is powerful because respondents appreciate knowing the results and respect the validity of the source: other retailers like themselves. Questions can be very simple, such as "Is your business stronger or weaker than last year?"

Surveys work because they set you apart from your competition. You're demonstrating that you care about the retailer's business. A poll is also a great way to capture names and contact information. It's also a great way to get retailers talking about you and returning to your booth, especially if you post the results daily during the show.

☞ The Daily Wrap – Review the Day

At the end of the day, you should have a short session with your booth staffers. Use this time to discuss the events of the day, identify any problems, go over upcoming events and strategies, and share the best suggestions of the day.

There are several good reasons for doing this: Daily meetings help ensure that the booth staff is on track and working toward common goals. Additionally, your reps will know that they are working for a company that constantly tries to improve itself.

The Five Key Points You Need to Know

Point Number One: Research Your Show Ahead of Time
Do all your homework before committing to a tradeshow. Make sure you're at the right show, in the right location, next to the appropriate vendors.

Point Number Two: Engage Attendees on Every Level
Exhibiting is a multi-dimensional experience. Consider how your retailers need to display your merchandise and set up your booth the same way.

Point Number Three: Use Signage Strategic use of signage can improve your tradeshow performance exponentially. Don't be afraid to recruit this silent salesman to highlight benefits, focus attention on a best seller, and introduce new lines.

Point Number Four: Giveaways Should Reinforce Your Brand The best promotional items teach your retailers how to be more effective, powerful salespeople. Consider merchandising tips, background information on your products, and selling techniques.

Point Number Five: Select Your Very Best People as Booth Staffers Booth staffers are your company's ambassadors at the show. Make sure to select your most engaging, enthusiastic employees who have great product knowledge and superlative sales skills.

How can I apply what I've learned?

CHAPTER EIGHT

At the Show
and After the Show

Laughter is the great social lubricant
that breaks down sales resistance.
— Rick Segel —

AT THE SHOW

☞ Make It Fun and They Will Come

We live in an entertainment-focused society. If you want to attract attention, you need to offer something fun, exciting, and entertaining.

This is why the best vendors build their booths the same way that a Broadway producer builds a set—and spends roughly the same amount of money! You can capture that same vibe of excitement and fun for far less money by using creative, playful signage throughout your booth.

Focus on the following:

- Interesting, readable fonts
- Color
- Creative copy

Make it look fun. Remember, content is king! Your words are your most powerful tool.

The electronic message board can be a great tool to implement a fun or playful strategy. Use it to flash fun quotes or a playful riddle with answers to follow. You can keep buyers at your booth—with your staffers and your merchandise!—as they wait for the answers to appear.

☞ Invite Your Buyers to Networking Events

Networking events generally occur after the tradeshow floor has closed for the day. Designed to gather industry professionals in an informal setting, these events often feature some sort of entertainment (a show or museum tour, for example) coupled with dinner and drinks. Take advantage of these opportunities.

"These aren't selling times," says Tony Orlando. "Think of networking events as a time to get to know your buyers and peers. It's a time to exchange ideas and just talk. Remember, you're focusing on forming relationships.

When everyone's sitting around and laughing and having a good time – that's when those relationships are forming."

Make a point of letting your customers know about the event. Personally inviting them and saying, "I'd love to spend more time talking with you" – without any added sales pressure! – is one of the highest compliments you can pay someone. In an increasingly impersonal world, you're taking time to recognize and engage with someone on a personal level, because you like them.

Remember, people do business with those people they like and trust. The easiest way to have someone like and trust you is to spend time getting to know them. Networking events are an ideal way to start that process.

☞ Cocktail Parties

Ask the show producer if you can host an after-hours cocktail reception in your booth for your accounts. Retailers love being invited to cocktail parties. It makes them feel important. Not only that, but cocktail parties can offer prime networking opportunities.

If you host the cocktail party in your booth, it should take place immediately upon the ending of the show. It should last no longer

If having the party at your booth is not a viable option, consider booking a hotel suite close to the tradeshow for this purpose. It can also serve double duty as a private meeting place for key accounts and staff meetings.

☞ Providing Networking Opportunities

Retailers don't always get the opportunity to know or socialize with other retailers. After all, they're in their shops most of the time. This gives savvy vendors a chance to be of real service to their customers. After all, they know lots of retailers. What could be easier than to set up a retailer-focused networking opportunity?

Plan to hold a networking dinner or breakfast, and ask someone — such as one of the speakers at the tradeshow— to help facilitate the networking. This may carry a modest fee but is well worth it. The networking process can have retailers offer opinions in response to a question of the whole group, or encourage retailers to ask each other questions.

☞ Power Networking

If you really want your networking event to be a winner, consider a technique called Power Networking. Line up two rows of chairs facing each other about four feet apart.

Have participants take a seat across from someone they don't know. They have five minutes to tell the person opposite them who they are, what they do, something interesting about themselves, and what they want to accomplish at the show. The facilitator announces when the five minutes are up, and the focus switches to the opposite person.

At the end of the second five minutes, the facilitator has the group change seats again so everyone is again facing someone they do not know. The process can continue for up to four rounds. Always leave time at the end so that brief connections can be built upon.

Power Networking is very popular with those retailers who need some kind of structure to thrive. Because there is a set format in place, some of the awkwardness of having to make small talk is removed.

☞ Ask Leading Questions

"Make it easy for your buyers," Stacey Heiss says. "Ask them leading questions: What products are you buying now? How well are the products moving for you? What works? What doesn't? You'll get some very honest answers. People don't hold back on the show floor."

For this reason, some vendors choose to view the tradeshow as a marketing resource. In addition to collecting anecdotal information like this, they want to collect demographic information about show attendees. Often, offering incentives is the best way to accomplish this: Attendees don't mind sharing information if they feel they're getting something of real value in return.

For the ultimate in information, remember to focus on open-ended questions. By encouraging attendees to answer with more than a "yes" or "no," you open up the dialog and move past the trite, polite answers to real, valuable content.

☞ Make It a Kodak Moment

Take a digital photo together with each of your customers and send it to them a week or so after the show. What could be of greater interest than getting a photo of oneself?

Having the sales rep in the photo standing next to the retailer is a great reminder of your company, especially with your booth's signage in the background.

☞ Can I Take a Picture?

It is common at a tradeshow for visiting retailers to ask to take pictures. This is especially common if you have an innovative display idea. Have a camera available for the use of those customers.

Granted, other vendors will ask the same thing, and their intentions are not as benign. However, focus on the positive. You can improve your sales by having a digital camera and printer on hand to give retailers pictures of the products they've bought and your displays.

☞ Honor Appointment Times

If you've made an appointment with a retailer to meet during the show, honor that appointment. One of the easiest ways to ruin a relationship and alienate a retailer is to schedule an appointment and then leave the retailer waiting. You're in essence saying, "I don't think you're important enough to keep my word to!"

Everyone runs a little late sometimes, but you should make every effort to be prompt. Don't keep your retailers waiting. Bear in mind that buyers will hesitate to make appointments with your reps for future shows if they are forced to wait. After all, they can't see the point—and can you blame them?

☞ Leaving Paper Incentives

Leaving paper refers to a buyer placing an order for the merchandise with the rep at the time of the presentation. This is getting increasingly difficult, so vendors must offer strong incentives.

Some vendors offer a 2-3 percent discount on an entire order if placed at the time of presentation. Others create a tier of discounts, allowing retailers to save 5 percent if they order at the time of presentation, and 2 percent if they place an order by the end of the show.

Retailers sometimes hesitate to place an order because they're not sure how much money is being spent. This is one of the times where you can use technology to your advantage. Use a laptop and computerized ordering techniques to complete the order when it is placed. You can check retailers' credit limits and let them know exactly how much they're spending. Work with your retailer to make it a solid order.

☞ Know the Score – Help Buyers Track What They Spend

Retailers often place numerous orders at a tradeshow, only to return to their stores and discover that they spent far more than they'd planned. Help them avoid this expensive buyer's remorse by creating a form and printing it on a card, which retailers can use to record their own running total of buying dollars spent.

Each line on the form should include vendor name, purchase order number, ship date, terms, and order total.

The back of the card can be imprinted with information about your company — a handy record that also leaves a reminder of your business in the buyer's pocket.

☞ Keep Your Booth Clean and Professional

If you walk through a tradeshow after the first few hours, you'd think a tornado had gone through the hall. There are papers everywhere, cups on the carpet, and food wrappers fluttering in the breeze. It's quite simply not attractive.

The way your booth looks tells something about you and your company. It's imperative to make sure that your booth remains clean and professional-looking throughout the entire event. Otherwise, you're not going to attract quality retailers.

If you are using a rep firm, make sure they understand and adhere to the standards you set. Doing so will help you to project a top-notch image — one retailers will feel more comfortable trusting their business to.

☞ Eliminate Distractions

"The reason you have staffers at the show," says Susan Friedmann, the Tradeshow Coach, "is to talk to attendees. There's no reason for them to be doing anything else!"

This includes newspapers, magazines, and the scourge of the tradeshow floor: cell phones. "Get that stuff out of there!" Friedmann advocates. Having these items in the booth for personal use turns off visitors. They also cause clutter, negating all of the effort you've put into designing and decorating your exhibit.

Additionally, if your staffers are occupying themselves with anything and everything but focusing on the show, it creates an impression that they don't want to be bothered with attendees. That's not the way to do business.

☞ Leverage Your Laptops

Laptops are a powerful distraction. With the web to surf and e-mail to check, less-than-motivated staffers can find a million things to do at the tradeshow besides engage with retailers.

Unless you are using a laptop to create orders, show catalogs of your product offerings, or run a pre-programmed PowerPoint presentation, don't have a laptop in your booth. Leaving the laptop behind also eliminates the chances of it "walking off " — with all of your sales data or other pertinent company information inside!

☞ Kids Are Customers, Too!

It varies by show, but in some industries, bringing the children to the tradeshow is very common. Make sure to have something in your booth for the children who are "along for the ride": Coloring books and crayons work for little ones, while video games keep the older kids happy.

If there are lots of children at your show, make sure that any refreshments you offer don't present a choking hazard. Additionally, a container of handi-wipes can help keep sticky fingers away from your merchandise.

☞ Make Tradeshow Specials SPECIAL

Tradeshow special deals are part and parcel of the exhibiting experience. Make sure your specials stand out by making an offer that is good ONLY at the show. Do not allow this offer to apply after the show. Doing so diminishes the importance of attending the show and "robs" the retailers who did place an order at the show. You lose credibility that way and damage your reputation with the retailers who feel shortchanged.

Some vendors offer additional savings for the first day of the show or for the first hour of the show. Other deals are saved until the end of the day, mid-week specials, and so on. The idea is to create activity during slower times and to build momentum.

☞ The Surprise Special

Hold special promotional offerings in your booth during the tradeshow. Consider having different unannounced specials in your booth at different times of the day to induce return visits.

Be creative when constructing these promotions. Try to anticipate anything that might make the buyer reluctant to leave an order. You might give a free gift with orders placed before 10 a.m., for example. Or—to encourage reorders at the same time a regular order is placed—you might offer a larger discount for doubling the quantity ordered of any style or model.

☞ Branding Means Consistency & Distinctiveness

Everyone understands the power of brands. We're a brand-driven society. The experience visitors to your booth have is an element of your brand.

Like the rest of your branding efforts, tradeshow exhibiting should be distinctive and consistent. This encompasses everything from the materials you hand out to the refreshments you serve. If you hand out cookies or candy, make them distinctive enough that your visitors will talk about them. One vendor has fortune cookies specially made for every show. Another has chocolate candies specially made in the shape of her logo, a large, feathery chicken! Believe me, people remember those candies.

Review every second retailers will experience at your booth, from the first hello to the last good-bye, including the ability to touch the merchandise. The experience they have will have a direct impact on their decision to purchase. The goal is to have the retailer not only buy your products but also say, "Company X has a great booth!"

🖙 No Loitering Here

Not every sales rep at a tradeshow is busy every single second. There's a tendency for reps to socialize. It's only natural. Tradeshow attendees understand that, but that doesn't make it any less off-putting.

There are few experiences more intimidating for a buyer than to encounter a group of three or more sales reps. This makes the retailer feel like an intruder, who is interrupting "the gang" with questions. You want your retailers to feel like welcome guests, not an annoyance!

Remind your team that there are plenty of networking and socialization opportunities that take place after the show closes for the day. Until then, however, they need to focus on welcoming and meeting the retailers.

☞ Never Drop One Customer for Another

There may be times at the tradeshow where you're working with a small account and a larger customer will stop by. As tempting as it may be, don't drop the smaller account to focus on the larger customer. It's bad manners and it will always come back to haunt you.

Additionally, although you might think that you're doing something nice for the larger account, you're really not. Large companies were once small companies, and they won't appreciate how you're treating the little guy. Respect is the most valuable commodity going. Don't throw it away needlessly.

☞ Card Collection Incentives

There's more to tradeshows than making sales. Not only are you forming relationships, you're also collecting information on your target audience. One reason to do this is simple: The more prospects we have, the greater the opportunity we have to sell. Another reason is a little more complex: Collecting and analyzing customer information will help vendors deliver the products and services more likely to appeal to their target audience.

Simply collecting cards is not enough. That's why tradeshow experts strongly recommend you do more than "give us your card for an incentive" collections. You want to know something about your attendees. Tie the incentive item to answering a brief survey, designed to discover something about the attendees' wants and needs.

☞ The Suggestion Process

Tradeshow attendees offer a broad pool of untapped ideas. Draw on their strength by asking retailers for their comments, ideas, and suggestions. A comment card is the easiest way to do this — and if you offer an incentive item in exchange, you'll have more suggestions than you know what to do with.

Ask specific questions on the comment card. For example, "What one thing could we do to make it easier for you to do business with us at the show?" Specific questions like this are far more likely to elicit useful answers than general "Tell us how we could do better" kinds of questions.

☞ Reward the Best Suggestions

People love to be recognized and they love surprises. Bond with your retailers by having them win competitions. A very simple competition can be built around the suggestion idea: Reward those retailers who give you great suggestions with a plaque.

Give retailers an engraved plaque that they can hang in their stores. Call it a "Creativity Award for Contributions to the Success of (Your Company Name)." Plaques are not expensive, and they can go a long, long way toward building community relations. When the retailer hangs up the plaque, people will talk about your company.

☞ Do You See What I See? Shopping the Competition

Tradeshows are one of the easiest ways to learn what's new and exciting from your competition. Don't sneak around trying not to look like a spy! Openly shop your competition. You'll be amazed at what you can discover.

At the same time, invite your competition to shop you. It's good business for both of you. You can't succeed without knowing what you're competing against.

☞ Interactive Contests Drive Traffic

Have a blackboard or whiteboard that announces the winners of each contest you hold throughout the day. By offering a daily drawing and posting the winners' names, you draw extra traffic to your booth.

The traffic makes your booth look busy. Retailers like to do business with busy companies. Your crowds are subtle yet effective validation of their decision to place an order with you. This effect is so strong that there are retailers who make a point of stopping at only the busy booths.

☞ Take a Walk

Accompany your better accounts on a walk around the show floor and let them point out what they are buying. Make sure to offer to buy them a soda or a coffee.

Listening to what they have to say demonstrates that you are interested in them, in their business, and the success of their store. You also gain a better understanding of their thinking. Again, you're strengthening a valuable relationship.

AFTER THE SHOW

☞ After the Order, I Still Love You

Follow-up is the single weakest area for most tradeshow exhibitors. Remember, your focus should be on relationship-building. If someone has placed an order with you at the show, this is a relationship you want to reinforce and strengthen.

Develop a method for following up with each retailer who placed an order at the show. It can be a simple phone call, e-mail, or thank-you note. Be sure to include an acknowledgment of what was ordered, thank the retailer for his business, and ask how sales are going. This is a nice personal touch that demonstrates that you're the type of vendor the retailer wants to do business with!

☞ Keep in Touch

According to Susan Friedmann, The Tradeshow Coach, every exhibitor should have a contact plan for after the show. "Even if someone didn't place an order at the show, you want to send them a thank-you note," she says. "Thank them for making the time in their busy day to see you."

Friedmann recommends prioritizing your leads and following up accordingly. "You have your hot prospects, your maybe prospects, and people who probably aren't prospects yet but are still good to know," she explains. "Thank everybody, and then make a point of getting in touch with hot prospects right away. Follow up with your maybes in about six weeks, and make sure to touch base with the others throughout the year."

This regular, friendly contact may just be enough to predispose the retailer to see you get the order the next time!

☞ Keep Your Promises

"If you make a promise at the show, you need to keep it," advises Heiss. Write these promises down and make sure not to lose the notes. "You might forget a promise, but you'd better believe that that retailer didn't forget." You may talk to 10,000 people during the course of the show, but even the busiest retailer will speak to only a few dozen. Your promise will loom large in their memory.

"Keep your word, and you're one of the good guys," Heiss concludes. "Forget it, and you look like you don't care about that company or their business."

☞ Give 'Em a Second Chance – Interactively

After the show, e-mail a special report to all the buyers who visited your booth and identify the five or ten best-selling items ordered during the show. Take a "I thought you'd want to know" approach.

If they purchased those styles or models, congratulate them. If they didn't, give them an opportunity to place an order for these styles. Make sure your e-mail tells them that this is a second chance to include these hot items in their order.

The Five Key Points You Need to Know

Point Number One: Treat Attendees with Respect Keep your booth clean and professional. Focus on one attendee at a time and never drop one customer for another. Eliminate distractions so your team is wholly focused on attendees' needs.

Point Number Two: It's the Relationship, Not the Sale! Focus on starting and maintaining long-term relationships with tradeshow attendees. That means you might spend more time networking and not sell as much merchandise right off the bat. That's okay. Sales come later. The relationship comes first.

Point Number Three: Keep Your Eyes Open Visit your competitors' booths. Listen to the questions that attendees are asking and what information excites them. What's important to people when they're in that booth will be important when they come to your booth.

Point Number Four: Embrace Suggestions Tradeshow attendees offer a broad pool of untapped ideas. Draw on their strength by asking retailers for their comments, ideas, and suggestions.

Point Number Five: Follow-up Is Essential The period immediately after a tradeshow is the prime time to start new relationships with the people you met at the event. Your competitors probably aren't doing this. Differentiate yourself by being the first person your attendees hear from after the event.

How can I apply what I've learned?

CHAPTER NINE

Group Purchasing

Price is what you pay,
value is what you get.
— Warren Buffet —

☞ What the Retailer Knows

Size really does matter. One independent retailer doesn't have a lot of buying power. Their orders generally aren't large enough to persuade major vendors to give them a break on price or more favorable terms, but if that one retailer joins forces with a group of peers, the situation changes.

At the same time, vendors have a hidden asset that is seldom noticed and rarely taken advantage of: their database of customers. These customers not only purchase your merchandise, but also like what you do or produce. These buyers or retailers all have similar wants, needs, and expenses. Your opportunity rests in that you know all of them, but they seldom know each other. Connecting them can be beneficial for both of you.

☞ What's It All About & How Can I Get Involved?

One of your hidden assets is your database of accounts, all of whom purchase similar services. All retailers buy packaging, fixtures, and display props.

If you become the conduit for bringing your retailers together for volume purchases and discounts, the suppliers of these products will even pay you for the opportunity to market to your customers.

The key is to be selective, and endorse only the products that you believe in and are good for your retailers. This is not the time to get greedy.

☞ Group Purchase of Web Designing Services

Group purchasing usually indicates reduced prices, but it can also make available expertise within an industry. Many retailers have trouble locating a web designer who understands the retail business.

As a manufacturer, you can contract for a package with a web design firm that specializes in retailing. In addition to the volume cost benefit for your retailers, they will be dealing with someone who knows their needs.

☞ Group Buying in National & Regional Magazines

A concept that is very popular in the bridal industry can easily be adapted for other industries. As a vendor you buy national ads and sell listings to the retailers that carry your product. Publications today can change the listing in an ad by geographical region so that a store in Texas is not listed in the New England edition.

The benefit to you is a very profitable business transaction, because the listings you sell to retailers more than cover the cost of buying the ads. In addition, the participating retailers purchase the feature merchandise. These ads pull so well that retailers are willing to compromise on the selection of merchandise you offer through this program.

☞ The Printing Opportunity

Printing is one of those functions in which quantity has a substantial impact on price. That's why any group purchasing or affiliate program that you initiate with printers will become mutually profitable for you and your retailers.

Some of the more popular items for group printing are signage, postcards, receipt books, service forms, purchase orders, and direct mail pieces.

If the Olympics can have an official printer, you can have one as well.

☞ Offer a Printed Catalog for Retailers to Buy

This concept has been around for years. Retailers buy catalogs from a buying group or a manufacturer to send to their customers. Although each retailer pays for the catalogs it buys, the cost is divided among so many retailers that the savings are substantial.

The only additional printing required is putting each individual store's contact information on the front and back of its catalogs, but that should not cost you any money.

To save you time, there are companies that will produce the entire catalog for you.

☞ The Thank-you Note

Upscale, high-ticket retailers like to show appreciation to their customers with thank-you notes. A service you can offer is the strategic alliance you form with a printer to make this gesture more cost effective for the retailer.

Offer your retailers several designs and allow them to buy these cards through you. It doesn't cost you any money and is a nice value-added service that shows you care about the retailers' business success.

☞ The Birthday Card

The birthday card is the number-one direct mail piece any retailer can use to create a lasting relationship with its own customers and diminish the typical leakage of customers. This service works the same as the thank-you note, but as an added benefit to retailers and you, the manufacturer encloses a gift with the birthday card: some type of coupon or special offer. (With a time restriction, of course!)

☞ Make a Hot Item Hotter in Full Color

Direct mail is still the number-one vehicle for retail advertising today, but retailers too often run out of ideas and material to send their customers. Nothing is more enticing than a photo of a hot item from the manufacturer. Full-color postcards with the store's logo printed on the card can be sold to the retailer at a nominal price, or charged against the co-op advertising account – or just given to the retailer.

☞ Create Local Advertising Groups

If you have several retailers located in the same trade area, assist them in creating group ads to increase their advertising power. Obviously, these stores should not directly compete with one another. They might be located in different towns but all carry a specific line.

☞ Supplying Store Fixtures

To create a brand presence in stores and help the retailers display your merchandise, offer incentives for free racks and fixtures. Incentives can be earned in numerous ways:

- From the retailer's purchase of a minimum amount
- From co-op dollars
- From a reduced price on a group buy

These fixtures generally have your company name on them. Even more important is for you to make these fixtures so distinctive that they are recognizable as yours even without your company name on it.

---

*In the business world
your rear view mirror
is always clearer
than your windshield.*
— Warren Buffet —

The Five Key Points You Need to Know

Point Number One: Be the Catalyst for Group Purchasing Help retailers unite so they can leverage better deals. You're in an ideal position to connect retailers who might otherwise never know each other!

Point Number Two: Unite Online Contract for a package with a web design firm that specializes in retailing and offer its services to a group of unified retailers.

Point Number Three: The Power of Print Group purchasing can make printing more affordable. Consider offering a catalog your retailers can use, especially if it's a catalog they can imprint with their own logo.

Point Number Four: Connect Your Retailers to Their Customers Make it easy for your retailers to send birthday and holiday cards to their customers.

Point Number Five: Supply Fixtures To create a brand presence in stores and help the retailers display your merchandise, offer incentives for free racks and fixtures.

How can I apply what I've learned?

CHAPTER TEN

Buying

Don't worry about the mule going blind,
just load the wagon.
— Rick Segel —

☞ What the Retailer Knows

This is where the rubber meets the road. Putting pen to paper to write the order is the actual moment when the retailer begins to spend money. If only it were that easy—for both parties—to make a simple decision about color, quantity, size, and delivery date. But that's not the case.

Retailers have buying habits—habits that aren't always in their best interests. Some buyers are very cautious, having been burned by bad decisions in the past. Others feel that the reps are out to "trick" them. Overcoming these barriers can be difficult, but it's not impossible. Again, the focus should be on education and working to help retailers improve their business. That way, everybody wins.

☞ Help Your Retailers Assess Their Buying

"Before I go in and meet with any of my store owners," says Dana Lurie, "I review their numbers. I look at the business they did last season, and a year ago. I try to track their sales. A lot of my retailers don't know how the lines they're selling are really doing. They don't know what's performing for them and what's not."

This is a very common tendency in some industries, where retailers tend to buy what they like personally. This can be very, very different from what sells, and quickly results in what Lurie calls the 85/15 rule. "Fifteen percent of their inventory is driving the business. The other 85 percent just sits there, costing them money."

Researching the sales numbers and tracking reorders may cost the rep a little extra time, but it can have a tremendous payoff. By doing this work, and encouraging reorders of strong-selling merchandise, a vendor can directly influence a retailer's inventory mix. If this new mix consists of proven sellers, both the retailer and the vendor will benefit!

☞ Introduce the Open to Thrive System

Retailers get themselves into trouble, not because they overbuy, but because they don't know they're overbought. Few retailers know what percentage of their sales they should be spending on inventory, how much should be allocated to expenses, and what percentage should be considered profit.

If you can introduce that to retailers, you'll completely transform their business. An easy way to share this information with your retailers is my Open to Thrive System.

The Open to Thrive System answers the age-old question How much inventory can and should I have? It will also tell your retailers if their expenses are in line. It works with actual invoiced costs, not retail selling dollars or markdown totals. This eliminates the chances for error.

Following the Open to Thrive System lets retailers know if they actually have the money they need to buy more inventory.

Open to Thrive is based on a very simple rule called the 40-55-5 Rule, which means that:

- 40 percent of the money made on sales will go toward expenses. It can be less but never more.

- 55 percent of the money made on sales will go toward new merchandise.

- percent of the money made on sales is Positive Cash Flow.

For more information on the Open to Thrive System, visit www.theretailersadvantage.com

☞ Know When to Say When

Every hot item cools off eventually, and as a rep, you're often the first person to know it. Don't keep this knowledge to yourself. Every retailer has turned a winner into a loser by ordering it once too often.

Help your retailers avoid this scenario by putting some type of system in place to alert them when an item is starting to slow. A retailer may still decide to order more at this point, but you've let them know sales are softening. They'll have made their choice with the best information you have to offer.

☞ Understand the Application Process

"What we've found, especially when dealing with our larger accounts," says Steve Wallace, of 1-800-GOT-JUNK, "is that they have a standardized, streamlined process to approve vendors."

This process is used to separate the credible, legitimate vendors from fly-by-night companies that don't deliver as promised or engage in negative business practices. "It's a way to demonstrate that you're at a given level. It makes them feel secure and comfortable doing business with you," adds Wallace. Wallace's company has a few employees devoted specifically to the task of vendor applications, but that may not be necessary for everyone reading this book. Simply having one or two people familiar with the vendor application process can save tremendous time and headaches.

The Five Key Points You Need to Know

Point Number One: Help Retailers Assess Their Merchandise Many retailers don't know what's selling and what's not: Take inventory and track sales to help them determine what's performing and what's not moving.

Point Number Two: Introduce the Open to Thrive System This simple system lets retailers know what percentage of their sales they should be spending on inventory, how much should be allocated to expenses, and what percentage should be considered profit.

Point Number Three: Know When to Say When Let your retailers know when a line is starting to slow or go cold.

Point Number Four: Understand the Application Process If you're trying to sell to an organization that has a standardized vendor approval process, discover what that process is and follow it—to the letter!

Point Number Five: Never Try to Trick Your Retailers There's nothing worse that the feeling a vendor has "sold you" a load of junk! Focus on education and working to help retailers improve their business first. The sales will follow!

How can I apply what I've learned?

CHAPTER ELEVEN

Super Secrets

*This may seem simple,
but you need to give customers
what they want,
not what you think they want.
And, if you do this,
people will keep coming back.*
— John Ilhan —

☞ What the Retailer Knows

There are two types of buyers in this world. To do well as a rep, you're going to need to be able to identify and deal with each type properly. After all, what appeals to Type A will fall flat with Type B. The sales tactics that appeal to Type B will be wasted on A. Let's look at each in turn and then discuss what motivates each type when they've got to make purchasing decisions.

Type A is the logical buyer. He approaches every purchasing decision armed with numbers. He knows what he wants to buy, how much he's willing to pay for it, how similar merchandise did for him before — often detailed by season — and that's that. He'll buy from the vendor who's selling what he wants to buy, at the price he wants to pay.

Selling to Type A is fairly straightforward. We're talking a real black and white deal here. The numbers are right or they're not. Decisions will be made largely on the prices you offer. I don't need to tell you how to sell to this guy. You already know.

Type B is a little group that I call Everybody Else. As you might suspect, this is a far larger group than Type A — I'd say Type B outnumbers Type A ten to one. Type B can be logical, but isn't necessarily. Other factors come into the purchasing decision besides price. Some of these reasons relate directly to you and how your company does business, while others are less tangible.

Your name might be Murray and the vendor's much-hated brother-in-law is also named Murray. Like it or not, on some level, that vendor is going to (probably unconsciously) hold that against you. There's not much you can do about that, short of changing your name (which I wouldn't recommend, unless it's a really, really, really big account).

Other reasons, however, are things you can do something about. These are the small issues that don't seem like anything to most reps, but can make a huge difference to the retailer. I talk to a lot of retailers while researching my books, and I always ask them what influences their decision to go with one vendor over another. Some of these answers might surprise you.

THE VENDOR OF CHOICE. . . Goes the Extra Mile

"There are times that in order to sell your product, you've got to do your part," says Lori Osborne. "There's a lot of extra work that comes with some of these promotions, and you've got to be there to help. I'm talking about the real nitty gritty stuff: helping set up the displays, put up the signage, you name it. Being ready to help out with the execution really matters."

It doesn't matter how big your customer is: They never have enough staff. From the largest chain stores to the mom & pop independents, there are never enough hands to move products, bring out stock, set up new displays, and so on. If a retailer has to choose between two promotions, and one comes with the expectation that the rep will do at least some of the work to get the program started while the other does not, that can make the choice much easier.

THE VENDOR OF CHOICE. . . Understands the Value of Fun

Increasingly, shopping has become an entertainment as much as a necessity. With anything and everything under the sun available for purchase online, consumers want something more than products presented in an appealing manner when they travel to a store. They want an experience.

Customers have a high regard for entertainment. Entertainment selling and a focus on fun are becoming very accepted ways of attracting and retaining customers. They come for a promise of a good time; they stay when that promise is fulfilled.

However, most retailers didn't come to the business straight from Broadway. They need some guidance on how to transform their stores into fun destinations. Reps who provide ideas, information, and formulas for using fun, humor, and play in the workplace can help retailers make their businesses more appealing.

Keep your eyes open constantly! Remember, you're on the road while the retailer is not. If you see a store that's using fun effectively, make a note of it. Combine this with information gathered from tip books, websites, newspaper articles, and so on, and pass them along to your retailers.

Finally, lead by example. If you're a fun person who can make doing business an enjoyable experience, that'll help. It's hard to take advice to lighten up from Serious Sid and Dour Dan.

THE VENDOR OF CHOICE. . .Is Easy to Get in Touch With

You would think this would be self-evident, but I can't tell you the number of retailers who have reps they can't easily contact. This is inexcusable, especially when keeping in touch is easier than ever before.

Provide your retailers with complete contact information: your office phone, your cell phone, your e-mail. It doesn't hurt to offer this information regularly and in different formats. Every piece of paper you leave with a retailer should have a way to contact you somewhere on it.

If any of your contact information changes, let your retailers know! Make a point of telling every single one of your contacts the new way to reach you.

There's nothing more frustrating for a retailer than to leave message after message — in a voice mailbox you never check because it's not current anymore! Update your messages, directing retailers to the proper way to reach you — or even better, use auto-forwarding technology to ensure you never miss a call.

Check your messages frequently. Steve Lang checks his e-mail at least twice a day, in an effort to remain in constant contact with his reps and retailers. Doing so can only improve your business.

THE VENDOR OF CHOICE...Communicates Appropriately

You want to be sure your retailers can reach you, but what happens when you need to reach them? Everyone has their preference, which often varies by the type of message being shared.

For one-on-one, rep to retailer conversation, you'll find that some retailers prefer a phone call while others want e-mail. Some want faxes, and a few still prefer in-person conversation. You'll want to make note of and honor this preference.

It's important to note that this may be very different from their preference for more general, company to retailer communication, such as company announcements, new campaigns, and so on. In this case, some retailers may prefer an announcement on the website, an e-mail, or direct mail. Again, you'll want to know.

"We try to use every channel possible to communicate with our customers," says Steve Wallace. "If they have a website or forum, we have a presence there. If they have a newsletter, global, national, or regional, we want to be in it. We participate in their conferences and go to the tradeshows. Wherever they are, we want to be there."

Ask your retailers what their preferences are. Many may have given the issue no thought, but for those who have, it's generally very important to them. More than one retailer has stopped doing business with a given vendor because they call too often!

THE VENDOR OF CHOICE...Offers User-Friendly Order Forms

There are fewer than 4,500 words in the U.S. Constitution: the single document that our system of laws comes from. Yet many manufacturer's order forms go on ten times as long, in miniscule type and incomprehensible legalese. This can alienate your retailers, who don't want to get tripped up by a clause they might not have seen, or accidentally agree to the one-sided "win/lose" position set out in many of these forms.

Eliminate this problem by developing an easy-to-work-with order form: easy to read, easy to understand, in a size that fits into a standard file folder. Go over this with each new account, taking the time to address any questions and concerns. This will eliminate the need to do so with each subsequent order.

THE VENDOR OF CHOICE...Is Willing to Put His Money Where His Mouth Is

"If you've got a great product, and you know it, and you want the stores to push it," says Sal Macaluso," you've got to be willing to do your part." Retailers consider how heavily a manufacturer is willing to promote a product before they commit their resources. "If you're not willing to do it," Macaluso continues, "why should they?"

When you meet with a retailer about a given campaign, come to the table prepared. Detail what your company is going to do to make the effort a success and how this will benefit the retailer. Many times, manufacturers are great at creating advertising that promotes their products but does little if anything for the store. If you can find a way that both parties benefit, you'll be in a much better position—one that will appeal to the retailers.

THE VENDOR OF CHOICE...Always Finds the Decision Maker

"In any organization, you're going to have a decision maker," Steve Wallace says. "That's the person you want to talk to." There's no cut-and-dried formula to discovering the decision maker. In some stores, it will be the owner, while other owners delegate all buying decisions to a trusted manager.

Identifying the decision maker is only the first step. "Spend time talking with this person," Wallace advises. "Learn what her objectives are, and what's important to her. She's the person you have to satisfy, so you really have to understand her before making any proposals."

THE VENDOR OF CHOICE...Knows Who the Most Important Person in the Store Is

The most valuable tool a manufacturer's rep or salesperson can have is a sense of proportion. No matter what happens, the most important person in any store is the customer. Without customers, there's no need for the retailer to place any orders with you or anyone else!

If you're working with a retailer in his store during normal business hours, there's a better than good chance that customers will come in. While retailers do understand that your schedule is busy, they also understand that customers are their bread & butter. Not all retailers can afford to have extra staff on hand to cover the sales floor while they're meeting with you. Graciously accepting that that is the reality of the situation is a sure way to put you in the retailer's good graces.

Nobody likes the prima donna rep who develops an attitude while waiting for the retailer to finish working with a customer. Waiting for an account is infinitely better than losing that account through impatience!

Also: Be helpful to customers who approach you. Even if you clearly don't work in the store, someone will most likely come up and ask where the restrooms are or if the sales flier's price applies to previous purchases. If it's a cut-and-dried question, and you know the answer, tell the customer. If it's a matter of policy or you don't know, walk the customer over to someone who can help her. It costs you nothing but a minute of your time and will impress customer and retailer alike.

THE VENDOR OF CHOICE...Realizes That Around Customers, Everyone Sells Everything

Picture this: You're waiting to meet with the retailer, and the store is packed. Every staffer is busy with a customer, and another customer is nearby, clearly in need of help.

What do you do?

If you're smart, you pitch in and help. No, it's not in your job description, but small efforts go a long way. Answering questions and being helpful will support the customer's goodwill. The customer doesn't realize that you're a sales rep. He just sees a person in the store who either treated him well or didn't. Your behavior will reflect not only on your company but on the retailer. You'll make yourself look good by making them look good.

The old I'm-just-a-sales-rep shrug might get you off the hook in the short run, but it will hurt you in the long run.

THE VENDOR OF CHOICE...Eliminates Surprises

Becoming the vendor of choice means building a strong relationship with your retailers: one built on trust and mutual respect. Don't jeopardize this relationship by attempting to fool your retailers or put one over on them. You should never leave the store feeling like you've fooled your customer or that you've gotten the better of the relationship. Instead, strive for deals that are mutually beneficial.

This means spelling things out. Make sure your retailers understand the deal before they sign on the dotted line (to the best of your ability). There should be no surprises, no hidden charges, and no undisclosed costs that will come back later to haunt both of you.

THE VENDOR OF CHOICE...Tells the Truth

Honesty is always the best policy. There's nothing retailers resent more than feeling like they've been lied to, either directly, when merchandise that arrives is nothing at all like what's been promised, or indirectly, when the merchandise they've ordered is exactly as promised — and exactly the same as what's selling at the mass market discount stores.

Whether it's lies of commission or lies of omission, telling untruths will always hurt you in the end. Retailers have limited tolerance for being fooled. More and more retailers are avoiding certain manufacturers because they've not been dealt fairly with, and they tell their colleagues and peers.

I'm not going to lie to you. There are times when being honest will cost you the sale. Your retailer might not want to stock a hot item if his competitor has also bought it. However, it's a matter of losing one sale versus losing a client. Look at the lifetime value of your customer. How much will you earn from him over the course of your career? Chances are that this number is much greater than any short-term gain you might make by making a sale that wasn't completely honest.

You really have to ask yourself Is the lie worth it?

THE VENDOR OF CHOICE. . . Fixes Mistakes

Everybody makes mistakes sometimes. You transposed two items on a sales form and instead of six stuffed kittens, your children's toy store got six sexy teddies. What do you do?

"You fix it," says Frank Epstein, who's been in the wine and liquor business since the '70s. "If I screw up, I'll do anything to fix it. If that means I send some merchandise for free, so be it. It's more important to repair the relationship with that retailer."

Admitting a mistake can be difficult, but it's rarely fatal. Owning up to an error and taking immediate steps to correct it can be the best thing you can do to reinforce your relationship with a retailer.

Retailers are humans themselves, and they understand how errors can happen.

THE VENDOR OF CHOICE...Discloses Discount Policies

Many retailers report that discovering a given retailer's discount policy is more difficult than discovering the Fountain of Youth. "Why," they ask, "do they hide this information?"

There's no good answer to that question. Time and time again, it's been proven that the vendors who have been open and fair with discounts, incentives, and price reduction policies fare much better than those who hide this information away. Withholding discounting information and offering discounts in a shady "back-room" fashion may create a mystique, but it also creates an impression of fundamental unfairness that many retailers resent.

Let retailers know what your company's discount policies are. Spell out the quantity levels needed for a discount, or if there are other criteria, such as paying promptly, anticipation, or timing considerations. This information should be easily found on your manufacturer's website, and it wouldn't hurt to have it printed out on a form your retailers can reference when doing their ordering.

THE VENDOR OF CHOICE...Opens a Showroom

"If you have all the components in place," Macaluso says, "you may want to consider opening a showroom. That way you've got salaried employees who are concentrating solely on your company and your products.

"All of your merchandise is in one place, adds Macaluso. "You can have everything in one location: the ability to take, process, and fill orders. All your follow-up can be right there. You'll be able to advise customers when their orders are shipping. It's the ultimate in customer service."

Showrooms work particularly well when they're conveniently located for the majority of your retailers. They're a favorite in those industries where bringing samples to individual retailers is difficult if not impossible! They do, however, require considerable time and a substantial investment, so consider carefully if you want to go the showroom route.

It's also important to remember the difference between a show-room and a storefront. Manufacturers who go into the business of dealing directly with customers soon realize that retailing is not where they want to spend their time and energy. Additionally, retailers often feel threatened when manufacturers effectively cut them out of the picture by selling to the public.

Keep your showroom for the trade, and let retailers sell to customers. That way, everyone enjoys the full benefits of the showroom, and you avoid the retailing headaches.

THE VENDOR OF CHOICE. . . Explains the Guarantees

Retailers are a cautious bunch. They'll feel better about buying from you if they know that there is some type of guarantee in place. Let them know that you stand behind your products.

Common types of guarantees between vendors and retailers include guarantees of quality, performance, and maintained markup. Additionally, guarantees that the merchandise delivered

---

will be an exact match of that displayed at the tradeshow or market are becoming increasingly common.

If you offer a manufacturer's guarantee to the customer, make sure that your retailers know this as well. This can often be the tipping point for a reluctant buyer, especially on a high-ticket item. Knowing that the product can be returned, refunded, or replaced will make it easier for the customer to say yes, which will make your retailer very happy indeed.

Guarantees are commonplace within the consumer world, and the trend has extended to the wholesale environment. Provide your retailers with complete information so that they know exactly where they stand.

THE VENDOR OF CHOICE... Has a Return Policy

Is there anything worse than opening up those boxes of broken, worn, or unwanted merchandise from your retailers? Perhaps not, but your retailers don't like getting returns any more than manufacturers do. However, retailers know that the easier they make the returns process, the more they keep customers' goodwill and encourage their repeat business.

Take catalog merchants, for example. Because they ship their merchandise with easy-to-use return labels, they get repeat orders. They have learned that making it easy for the customer to do business with them pays off.

Take a page from the catalog merchant. What can you do to instill your retailers with that same level of confidence when they do business with you? Consider your return policy. Is it easy for your retailers to process returns, or does it quickly become more trouble and time than it's worth?

Manufacturers often lie about their return policy. This is a prime opportunity for you to differentiate yourself from your competitors: Spell out an honest and fair return policy…and abide by it. This alone can help you build your brand!

THE VENDOR OF CHOICE…Has an Order Cancellation Policy

This is a topic that no one wants to talk about. However, it needs to be addressed. Of course, you don't have to spend time going over your cancellation policy with each retailer. However, you should clearly state your policy, distinguish between canceling part or all of an order, and specify the steps a retailer needs to take to make a return properly.

Here are some areas to consider covering in your policy statements:

• Can an order be canceled?

• What penalties might there be for cancellation?

• What if the vendor does not ship the order by the completion date?

If orders are being placed using the retailer's own order pad, the vendor should produce a statement for retailers to read about cancellations. If the manufacturer's order form is being used, the cancellation policy should be clearly stated on it in "readable" language.

THE VENDOR OF CHOICE...Has a Return Policy

What is the manufacturer's policy on returning merchandise? Similar to the issue of damaged merchandise, your policy on returns must be clearly stated. Retailers simply need to know their options.

Here are some concerns to address in your policy:

- Can a retailer return merchandise?
- What is the time frame for even inquiring about a return?
- How do you handle time-sensitive or seasonal merchandise?
- Can slow sellers be substituted for different styles?
- How do you handle a government recall or manufacturer recall of a product?

THE VENDOR OF CHOICE...Has a Damaged Merchandise Policy

Damaged merchandise isn't fun for anybody, but it's a fact of life. The major concern voiced by retailers about damages is simply not knowing what the company policy is.

Counter this by letting your retailers know your policy well in advance. State it clearly on the purchase order. If the retailer is using his or her own order pad, state the policy on a fact sheet. Post it on your website.

Here are some of the questions that retailers like answered:

- Do I have to get a return authorization?
- What is the waiting period for an authorization label?

- Will you credit the return before the goods are actually returned, and will doing so cause any problems?

- Can the product be destroyed in the field or only in transit?

- Can your field sales rep handle this?

THE VENDOR OF CHOICE...Discloses Use of Discounters & Mass Merchants

No retailer can ever fault a vendor who chooses to sell the same merchandise to discounters or mass merchants. However, there's not a single small retailer out there who is thrilled when they discover that "their" merchandise is being sold at bargain basement prices across town.

Retailers work hard to protect the integrity of their stores and their prices. They just want to know who their competition is. It behooves you to be honest with your accounts. If a given line is being sold to a discounter, let them know. There is nothing worse than repressing that information. You might win the battle, but you will surely lose the account.

THE VENDOR OF CHOICE...Discloses Online and Non-Traditional Competition

Online and non-traditional retail outlets are here to stay. Most retailers are aware of this, but have little to no understanding about how the e-commerce phenomenon affects their business nor how they can compete.

The first key to helping your retailers is raising awareness. Just as retailers have the right to put manufacturers' merchandise on their websites, manufacturers have the right to list all the ways that consumers can get their products. To keep the goodwill of your retailers, keep them informed. This will prevent them from being blindsided by customers saying, "Oh, I can get it cheaper on Amazon.com."

THE VENDOR OF CHOICE...Explains Their Factory Outlets and Selling Direct Online

Retailers need to know the same information about factory outlets as they do about discounters and mass merchants.

They should also be prepared to lose some of their retail customers when manufacturers choose to market merchandise in this manner. So let your retailers know if you have your own stores, and if so, where they are located and what types of merchandise they carry. Sometimes your retailers can be hurt just by the name of the outlet. Even if it doesn't hurt them directly, it becomes an unnecessary annoyance. Inform your retailers. Don't forget to let them know of any upcoming plans to add a new outlet.

Retailers must be able to make intelligent decisions about doing business with vendors they compete with. Frankly, on some level, vendors selling directly is a dirty pool: There's no way your retailers can compete. If you want to incorporate online sales without fundamentally damaging your relationship with your retailers, consider services like www.shopatron.com, which funnels online sales to local retailers.

THE VENDOR OF CHOICE...Knows Who They Are

Have information readily accessible so the retailer can know exactly who the target audience is for a given line of merchandise. Using either demographic or psychographic information, show your retailers where your product fits.

THE VENDOR OF CHOICE...Caters to the Convenience Customer

The strongest and most loyal customers are the convenience customers. These customers remain loyal to those businesses that are the most convenient to them.

Convenience is more than location. Convenience is the ease of doing business. It is also about saving time, not necessarily about saving money. People will pay for convenience, whether it's the consumer who wants the ready-made grab-and-go sandwich or the retailer who knows that he'll get a complete set of promotional materials if he orders your merchandise.

Explore every aspect of your contact with retailers to simplify and speed up the process.

THE VENDOR OF CHOICE...Knows Their "A" Customers

Customers can be divided into three groups: those who spend a lot, those who order constantly, and those who recently did business with you. As a vendor, you need to know who these customers are and what category they represent.

At the same time, the most important customers sometimes fall through the cracks. These are the steady, consistent, loyal customers who might not spend a lot of money, don't place a lot of reorders, or haven't placed an order for a few months. Yet your merchandise is always in their stores, and their orders are placed on a consistent basis.

Know your favorite customer types and decide how you value them.

THE VENDOR OF CHOICE... Remembers the Human Factor

"Business is violent," says Stephen Situm of Stephen Vincent Wines. "When you get right down to it, business is the exploitation of human beings: their labor, their energy, you name it. But you don't have to make it worse than it has to be.

"Remember to treat everyone with dignity," he adds. "This extends to how you do business. Think about it:

If you're giving super discounts to the large chains, for example, then you're shifting that cost onto the smaller retailers. The little guy is continually getting hurt. If you think about that, and what that means, you might change how you do your discounts.

"Will you build a larger business that way? I don't know — but you'll build a better one."

THE VENDOR OF CHOICE... Knows How to Be the Bottom-line Resource

Many vendors talk about being the bottom-line resource for their retailers — the one the retailer consistently makes money with. But from the perspective of the smaller retailer, there seems to be more talk than concrete program.

Major stores can and do dictate to manufacturers the maintained markup they expect, or they will discontinue carrying the line. This forces the manufacturer to supply markdown money, additional advertising allowances, or off-price goods. It is time that these benefits are offered to the smaller retailers who are loyal accounts.

Formalize a guaranteed markup program and offer it to stores that qualify. The qualifications might include:

- Approved computer systems
- Minimum requirements of inventory
- Advertising budgets
- Store reputation

With such a program, a real benefit for you is the shift in focus from price to performance. This is a much healthier way to do business, and it creates a true vendor/retailer partnership.

THE VENDOR OF CHOICE...Stresses Call Center Courtesy

You spend money to employ the best salespeople, have a beautiful tradeshow booth, and produce the best possible merchandise. Maintain that high level of service by having the personnel who answer your telephones and communicate in other ways with your customers be well-trained, responsive, and compassionate. Even a slow-paying retailer deserves courtesy and respect.

THE VENDOR OF CHOICE...Knows That Manners Matter

"Manners might seem old fashioned, but they never go out of style," says Frank Epstein. "Be considerate. Take off your hat in elevators. Don't smoke. Move to the back or side of the elevator to let others get on. Turn off your cell phone — and don't make or take calls when you're in someone else's company."

Manners are important. Your behavior reflects not only on you, but on your company. If you feel that your etiquette might be lacking, there are guides online and in bookstores, as well as classes that can help you brush up.

THE VENDOR OF CHOICE...Knows It's the Thought That Counts

What is an appropriate gift for a vendor to give a retailer? Most retailers are not looking for a tangible gift from a vendor. Their gift is the quality service your company offers, coupled with promotions when available and good follow-up.

Most buyers do not like being put in the position of making decisions because someone has given them a nice gift. This has recently been demonstrated in the pharmaceutical industry, where doctors felt incredible pressure to prescribe certain drugs after manufacturer's reps lavished them with expensive gifts.

Keep things in proportion. Send a thank-you note for orders, or buy the staff a snack tray or candy assortment that everyone can share. These touches give the message that you appreciate doing business with them and are acknowledging the end of another year together — without trying to buy their business with a gift.

THE VENDOR OF CHOICE... Knows the Importance of Inventory

You can't sell what you don't have. Retailers make more money when they have the goods. The greatest deal in the world is worthless if retailers have to wait a month to get the merchandise. Their customers are used to instant gratification, and if they're told they have to come back another day, they won't come back at all.

To serve your retailers better, watch the performance of the smaller regional vendors who compete successfully against much larger competitors by changing the playing field. Instead of focusing on price, they concentrate on "in stock" inventories that allow the retailer to place more "at once" orders.

The other industry where doing business with a stock house has always been an advantage has been the catalog business. Catalogs have always been more concerned with back-up inventory than having the goods available. With more and more retailers being forced into multi-platform retailing and a web presence, the vendor who has the merchandise readily available is becoming more valuable than ever before.

THE VENDOR OF CHOICE... Teams Up – Joins Forces with State Retail Associations

Every state has a state retailers association. Its goal is to improve retailing within the state. When the retailers' business is good, the vendors' business is generally good. These associations offer wonderful opportunities to meet and partner with retailers.

All it takes is a phone call or e-mail to a state association to ask how you can be involved and what committees you can serve on. Becoming involved is the most effective way to network. It will make you stand apart because very few vendors get involved. The ones who do reap big rewards.

Perhaps the most important benefit a vendor can realize by joining the retailers association is that it becomes easier to think like a retailer. Being regularly exposed to the thoughts, feelings, and concerns of your retailers helps you understand them better — and the better you understand your retailers, the more effectively you'll be able to sell to them.

THE VENDOR OF CHOICE. . .Helps Retailers Hire the Best

Finding good people is a struggle for most retailers. Help your retailers start the process with a job application form that reflects more effective content than most retailers have the time to develop themselves. Create a job application outline to illustrate the better questions to have on applications, such as:

- What special talents do you bring to our store?
- What do you see yourself doing six months from now?
- What was your biggest accomplishment at your last job?
- What would your last employer say about your work?
- If you could change one thing about your last job, what would it be?
- Why did you select our store as a place to apply for work?

THE VENDOR OF CHOICE...Can Act as a Matchmaker When a Store is for Sale

Vendors can be the perfect conduit for bringing store buyers and sellers together. If a store is to be sold, it is in the vendor's best interest to see it sold to a retailer who does business with that vendor.

Many stores have been sold to companies that have their own resources, causing a long-term account to be lost overnight because of new ownership. You're literally back at square one.

Instead, try to be a matchmaker. Finding someone you already have a relationship with to buy a store that's on the market allows you to continue a profitable relationship. It is clearly to your advantage.

THE VENDOR OF CHOICE...Offers Category Management Consulting

Category management is an innovative way to help retailers view their merchandise. This practice is based on the realization that there are many different types of merchandise, and each type has a specific role to fill within the store.

For example, there is destination merchandise: the products customers will drive many miles, past other stores, to purchase in a specific location. Image enhancer merchandise is the merchandise a store has to carry to WOW the customer, while turf protector merchandise consists of the items that are almost "required inventory" for a store in that specialty.

The point is to have a good balance of the different types of merchandise. Rather than one set of hard numbers, it's critical that a retailer is aware of how his store is set up, and what the category mix looks like at any given time.

However, this kind of analysis is beyond most retailers. Consider hiring a consultant to work with your accounts and train them in this effective, powerful way to buy inventory.

"Did you see this?"
are the most powerful sales words
anyone can ever use.

The Five Key Points You Need to Know

Point Number One: Make It Fun We like to do business with people who are fun. Retailers spend a lot of time every day with people in less-than-great moods. Make your visit or call something they can smile about.

Point Number Two: Be Easy to Contact Make sure your retailers can get you when they need you. Share your e-mail, cell phone number, direct line number, and other contact information with all your retailers—and keep it updated!

Point Number Three: Focus on What's Important to Your Retailer Around the customer, everyone sells everything. Whenever you're in a retailer's store, make sure you remember that making the customer happy is the first priority.

Point Number Four: Eliminate Surprises Tell the truth, disclose terms, and make sure your retailers never feel blindsided by the terms of the contract they just signed. It's your job to make sure they're fully informed.

Point Number Five: Fix Mistakes Mistakes happen to everyone. Handle yours quickly and professionally—and don't stop fixing it until the retailer is satisfied.

How can I apply what I've learned?

The People Behind
The Book

In an industry as dynamic and ever-changing as retail, no one person can know everything! I'd like to thank those retailers and sales professionals who were good enough to share their expertise for this book. Their collective wisdom, good humor, and industry insight were really an inspiration! Special thanks to:

Angelo Marzocchi, Angelo Marzocchi Associates

Dana Lurie, Mon Cheri LLC

Frank Epstein, Wine Sellers of America

Linda Rigano, ThomasNet

Lori Osborne, ConAgra Foods

Mike Green, Amesbury Chairs

Paul Gerbino, ThomasNet

Sal Macaluso, eFashion Central

Stacey Heiss, Western Exhibitors

Stephen Situm, Stephen Vincent Wines

Steve Lang, Mon Cheri LLC

Steve Wallace, 1-800-Got-Junk

Susan Friedmann, The Tradeshow Coach

Tony Orlando, George Little Management

Rick Segel

Rick Segel, CSP, a seasoned retailer of 25 years, owned one of New England's most successful independent women's specialty stores. He is the marketing expert for Staples.com, a contributing writer for numerous national and international publications, and a founding member of the Retail Advisory Council for Johnson & Wales University. Rick is the Director of Retail Training for the Retailers Association of Massachusetts. He is the creator of the Retailers Association of Massachusetts Awards of Excellence Program (RAMAEs) that has recognized over 50 of the most innovative retailers in the state.

Rick is currently serving on the Boards of Directors for five corporations and associations. Rick developed and authored The Retail Technology Assessment and The Retail Store Assessment for Microsoft's retail technology division. Rick recently launched his boldest initiative by creating The Retailer's Advantage, a membership website devoted to helping independent retailers improve their businesses.

Rick holds the CSP (Certified Speaking Professional) designation from the National Speakers Association, an elite rank held by only 7 percent of professional speakers. Rick is a past president of the New England Speakers Association, and he has been a featured speaker in 49 states and on four continents, delivering over 1,900 presentations.

Rick has authored nine books, two training videos, and a six-hour audio program. *Retail Business Kit for Dummies*, published by Wiley, Inc., became the #1 selling retail how-to book in the United States in January 2002 and is now in its second edition. *Laugh & Get Rich: How to Profit from Humor in any Business*, published by Specific House, has been critically acclaimed as a must-read for its insightful outlook at our entertainment-based society and has been translated into Japanese, Chinese, and Korean. *The Essential Online Solution: The Five Step Formula for Small Business Success*, published by Wiley, Inc., is a primer for business owners on creating e-commerce success. He is also the author of *Rick Segel's Retail Inventory Control Solution: Open to Thrive* and *The 5,000 BEST Sale & Promotional Names & Ideas Ever Compiled*, and coauthor of *Retailing in the 21st Century*. Most recently, he authored *The Art and Science of Creating Powerful Promotions and Sensational Sales* and *Becoming the Vendor of Choice: The Secrets to Powerful Retail Relationships*, both published by Specific House.

Rick has also appeared on TV, radio, and in many print articles. His down-to-earth, street-smart approach to business makes him a crowd pleaser wherever he goes.

For more information about Rick Segel, please visit
www.RickSegel.com.

Rick Segel's RESOURCES FOR RETAILERS

- **Make your store a profit-producing machine**
- **Pro-active retailing ideas that WORK**
- **I use a laugh-and-learn approach that is easy to understand and apply**

Retail Business Kit for Dummies 2nd Edition

Ranked #1 Retailing book at About.com

This 408-page book is the most complete guide to retailing today. Includes a CD-ROM of forms, check lists, and guides.

$34.95

The Essential Online Solution

The 5-step formula for small business success. The fastest and easiest way to e-commerce.

$22.95

Laugh & Get Rich

Learn how to profitably use the tool of humor to increase your bottom line. In its sixth printing.

$19.95

Powerful Promotions and Sensational Sales

This how-to, step-by-step manual reveals the secrets of sale professionals and will increase your sales results significantly.

$29.95

The 5000 BEST Sale & Promotional Names & Ideas Ever Compiled

The name says it ALL!

$19.95

Becoming the Vendor of Choice

A collection of tips and techniques for vendors to create profitable relationships with retailers.

$19.95

Retail Inventory Control Solution

Open To Thrive — A revolutionary way to look at Open to Buy, 1 CD-ROM and a tracker for sales, inventory, and cash flow.

$29.95

Audio CD: How to Make Your Retail Business Profitable

(the complete 6-CD package) Explores every aspect of the retail business for profitability.

$59.95

Video: Stop Losing Sales

The perfect training video for sales personnel and their managers.

$39.95

Video: Effective Suggestive Selling

Did You See This?—Increase sales and sales e ectiveness while you enjoy the process.

$39.95

Retail Sales Bible, The GREAT Book

GREAT is the acronym for the ultimate system for retail selling. G: greeting, R: research, E: experimenting, A: additional items for multiple sales, T: tether the customer back to the store by collecting data.

$19.95

System: How to Run a Sale

The most comprehensive tool to create legendary sales that produce amazing results. This system delves deeper into the art and science of running sale promotions.

A service whose time has come!

The Retailer's ADVANTAGE

All the expertise you need is only a mouse-click away.

The Retailer's Advantage is the newest concept in retail education and networking. This membership service shares the insider secrets, tactics, tools, and strategies needed to draw more customers into your store and persuade them to buy more than they planned or you even expected them to buy.

The Retailer's Advantage offers resources to motivate you and your sales.

- **Live (online) events** including, weekly live interviews with the movers, shakers, and advisors to who's who in retailing, reviews of member websites, round-table discussions, interactive Q & A programs, and tech talk with our web guru.
- **Tools to use**. "Open to Thrive" inventory control system, a promotion finder, a resource for newsletter articles, an Ask the Pro section, and more.
- **How-to articles** and an archive of audio and video programs.
- **A community of retailers** sharing information with each other.

Join our community now. Even if you implement just one great idea, your subscription will more than pay for itself.

Sign up today for **The Retailers Advantage** at **$49.95 per month.**
There are NO Contracts to Sign, NO Time limits, and if you aren't happy —
but we know you will be — you can cancel at any time.

Nothing could be easier and risk free.

Please visit **www.TheRetailersAdvantage.net**
to see for yourself.